To Mom

Location
of Walks

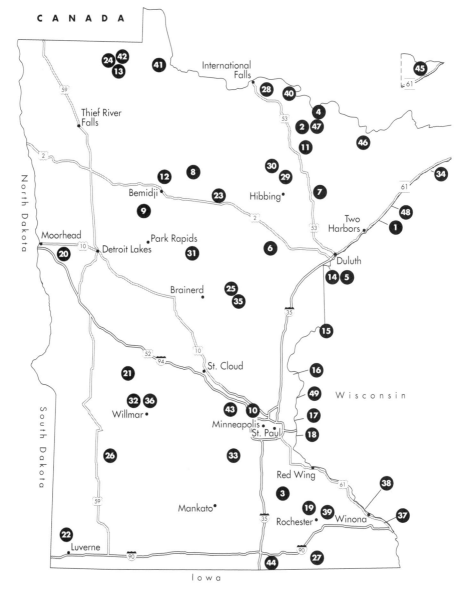

Contents

Riverside Rambles

Prairie Paths

Hikes into History

Strolls among Wildlife

The Hikes at a Glance

	Large tracts of big trees	Prairie/meadow	Lake	River	Waterfall	Wilderness	Overlook/vista	Wildlife/birds	Historic significance	Bog/wetland
1. Split Rock River Gorge				■	■	■	■	■		
2. Vermilion Falls				■	■		■		■	
3. Hidden Falls and Fawn Trails				■	■					
4. Vermilion Gorge			■	■	■		■		■	
5. Grand Portage Trail				■					■	
6. Savanna Portage Trail				■					■	■
7. Big Aspen Trail	■							■		
8. Lost Forty Trail	■			■					■	
9. Mississippi Headwaters/Schoolcraft	■		■	■					■	
10. The Learning Trail			■							
11. Orr Bog Walk				■				■		■
12. Lake Bemidji Bog Walk			■							■
13. Hayes Lake Bog Walk										■
14. Silver Creek Trail				■	■		■		■	
15. Two Rivers Trail				■				■		
16. River Trail				■				■		
17. Riverside Trail				■						
18. N. Railroad Grade/Backpacking Loop		■		■			■			
19. Third Bridge to Second Bridge				■						
20. Around the River Hike		■		■				■		
21. Kame and Kettle Walk		■					■	■		■
22. Cliffline and Upper Mound Trails		■					■	■		
23. Cut Foot Sioux/Simpson Creek Trail	■		■					■	■	
24. Homestead Trail		■							■	
25. Ogechie Lake			■						■	

This guide points out important features and sights of each hike in the book that will help you. A hike is marked only when the attraction is significant. For example, you'll see wildlife on all the hikes, but you're more likely to encounter uncommon or large numbers of wildlife on the hikes indicated here.	Large tracts of big trees	Prairie/meadow	Lake	River	Waterfall	Wilderness	Overlook/vista	Wildlife/birds	Historic significance	Bog/wetland
26. Mazomani's Prairie Hike		■		■			■	■	■	
27. Zumbro Hill Cemetery Hike									■	
28. Echo Bay Trail						■	■			
29. South Dark River Hiking Trail				■			■	■		
30. Sturgeon River Trail				■			■			
31. Shingobee Recreation Area Trail							■	■		
32. Pondview Interpretive Trail		■	■					■		■
33. Lawrence Headquarters Loop				■						
34. Oberg Mountain Loop							■			
35. Observation Tower Hike							■			
36. Mount Tom Overlook							■			
37. Seven Overlooks Hike		■		■			■			
38. Riverview Trail				■			■			
39. Dakota to Meadow Trail				■			■			
40. Blind Ash Bay Trail			■				■	■		
41. Levee Walk			■					■		
42. Pine Ridge Trail and Dam Walk		■	■							
43. Bjorklund Lake Hike			■							
44. Big Island Trail	■		■							
45. Eagle Mountain Trail			■			■	■	■		
46. Bass Lake Trail			■			■	■	■		
47. Herriman Trail			■	■		■	■	■		
48. Shovel Point and Beach Trails			■				■			
49. Pothole Trail				■			■			

Introduction

A couple of years ago, when I was finished writing my first book about hiking, *Great Wisconsin Walks*, I reflected on how much I enjoyed walking the trails and how much I had learned about the area. Yet I was glad that the job was over because a great deal of work goes into any book, and especially one that deals with an entire state. Then, when the Wisconsin book was well received, and even won a couple of awards, my publisher approached me about doing a book on great walking spots in Minnesota.

I had to think about my answer. After all, Minnesota is a big state, something I appreciate even more now that I've traveled over 8,000 miles getting from one destination to another searching for great walking adventures. Actually, Minnesota's 84,064 square miles qualify it as the nation's twelfth largest state. Yet I was never really close to telling Wisconsin Trails no. I love hiking and the places it takes me.

I can honestly say that I have traveled to every corner of Minnesota looking for great walking and hiking places. And I found a lot of them, many located within state parks. Part of the reason is that there are so many state parks—63 at last count—and that they were established to preserve unique and beautiful places. Other fine walking spots are located in one of Minnesota's two national forests, the Chippewa and the Superior, and within many of the 56 state forests. Still others are found in numerous county parks, most of them small in area when compared to their state park counterparts but often equally impressive.

Picking trails for inclusion in this book was difficult. Not only does Minnesota contain countless trails spread out over 84,000 square miles but also each trail changes with the season, the last storm, and people's use of it. In the end, my criteria were subjective. If I liked my experience on a trail, I probably included it here.

There were a few exceptions to this rule. Some treks that I loved are not included here because, for example, no maps were available or bad weather prevented me from taking legible notes. Some of the spots I wish I could have written about include Lake Bronson State Park, Pipestone National Monument, Banning State Park, Camden State Park, Quarry Hill Nature Center, Fort Ridgely State Park, and several parks along Lake Superior, as well as sections of the Superior Hiking Trail.

For instance, Lake Bronson State Park, in the far northwest corner of Minnesota, is a wonderful place, with lots of trails. It boasts a unique ecosystem, a place where the prairie meets the North Woods. Unfortunately, when I visited the park, it was in the midst of a major trail rerouting, and the written information and map didn't match the new trail system.

So just because I failed to include a place doesn't mean that it's a bad walk. But rest assured, if I did include a spot, I enjoyed my hike there and it's likely you will too. If your favorite trail is left out, send me a letter (c/o Great Minnesota Walks, Trails Media Group, P.O. Box 5650, Madison, WI 53705) and I'll check it out for the next edition.

Also, I may have hiked only a small part of the available trails at any one location. The maps included in the book reflect only the general area where the hike occurs and are as accurate as I felt they needed to be to help you enjoy your walk. Distances are approximate, as is the listed time it takes to hike a particular trail. Don't hesitate getting the park map or other reference and striking out on your own. Discovery is one of the delights of hiking.

A word about hiking verses walking. What's the difference? Not much really. Both involve the same muscles and the same type of coordination. The usual dictionary definitions indicate that hiking involves greater distances than walking. Perhaps the most telling difference is the location in which the activity occurs. We walk when we shop or go to the store. We walk the dog around our neighborhood. Hiking, on the other hand, usually means trudging in the great outdoors along rugged and tree-lined paths, more or less removed from urban constraints. Yet there are parks inside many cities that could well qualify as great hiking spots. Several of Minneapolis's large urban parks or Duluth's Lester Park come to mind.

For purposes of definition, I've used the words *hike* and *walk* interchangeably in this book, even though the title includes only one of them. Nonetheless, the important thing is that the book contains a wide variety of walks (or hikes) that will appeal to most people who want to experience the wonders of Minnesota's vast network of parks. Our title contains the word *walks*, at least partly because we don't want to give the impression that the book is only for the long-distance hiker. There are some very tame hikes included here, some less than a mile in length.

A couple of additional words about hiking are in order here. It's something almost everyone can do, and it doesn't require special equipment. Shoes are important, but on most of the walks in this book, good, comfortable running or walking shoes will work fine. Sometimes, on the more remote hikes, in more rugged areas, hiking boots will be better choices.

One piece of equipment that is invaluable, especially if you plan to tackle some of the longer hikes, is a compass. While most of these hikes are pleasantly straightforward and along well-used and marked trails, some flirt with very wild country. If you lose your way, a compass could make the difference between a little inconvenience and serious discomfort—or worse. In order for a compass to do you much good, you also need a sense of where you want to go. Always know what direction you would head in if you got off the trail and lost. For instance, always be aware of the direction or heading you would assume to reach the nearest road. And, unless you are expert with a compass, don't aim for a tiny target, like a parking area, but rather for a long stretch of road or the shore of a large lake.

I hope that the organization of the book into types of walks makes it easy to use and versatile. Feel like viewing some majestic waterfalls? Looking for magnificent trees that are older than any person on earth? Want great views of a variety of terrains and bodies of water? Check out the individual sections in the book to help you choose. The guide at the beginning of the book will also help you select a walk. It lists additional sights you'll see along each of the walks. Finally, the map of Minnesota pinpoints the location of each hike mentioned in the book.

The maps of the individual walks in the book were drawn to provide stylized renderings that approximate distances between the actual sites. As artistic pieces, they recall the days when map-making was an art long before it was a science. The map artist, Pam Harden, who worked with me on *Great Wisconsin Walks,* has sketched some wonderful two dimensional renderings that feel as if the third dimension is present.

So get on with it. Hit the trail and enjoy some of the wonderful places Minnesota has to offer.

Waterfall Walks

1

Split Rock River Gorge
Split Rock Lighthouse State Park

Distance: 4.5 miles

Time: 3 hours

Path: An obvious, well-worn path filled with dirt, rocks, and roots. The elevation at the wayside where the hike begins is approximately 620 feet above sea level, and the overlook is at about 900 feet. But don't be fooled. You'll hike up and down enough small hills and ravines to tally well over a thousand feet of elevation change.

Directions: From the entrance to Split Rock Lighthouse State which is at milepost 46 on Highway 61, go southwest approximately 2 miles to the Department of Transportation wayside on the right.

Contact: Split Rock Lighthouse State Park, 3755 Split Rock Lighthouse Road, Two Harbors, MN 55616; (218)226-6377.

Highlights: Many waterfalls, a panoramic view of Lake Superior, lots of birch, aspen, and alder, and some challenging elevation changes.

Most of this hike is on the Superior Hiking Trail and within the boundaries of the state park. Begin at the southwest end of the wayside, where there is a map board. The half-mile-long spur trail leading to the Superior Hiking Trail winds through a birch forest that also contains some aspen and fir. Full-dimension wood planks and, later, split logs help you cross wet spots. As the highway sounds recede, you can begin to see the river gorge on the right. The alder are treelike, with trunks the size of a human calf. Along with mountain maple, the alder comprise much of the understory.

A trail sign sits at the junction with the Superior Hiking Trail. If you turn left, you'll have a 4.3-mile hike to Gooseberry Falls State Park. But you'll want to turn right, toward what the sign says is the Split Rock River Crossing. There is a steep descent down to a little creek and a bridge that crosses it. The uphill climb beyond the bridge is on wood and earth steps, past a big balsam fir tree on the left, 16 inches in diameter and about 85 feet in height.

Soon you'll hear the first of many waterfalls. Although trees partially block the view, you can see white water cascading down reddish bedrock into the river gorge. Less grand but equally impressive is a

stand of bunchberry
(*Cornus canadensis*)
located on the left as
the trail loops left and
up a steep hill. This
aggregation of small
plants is wonderful. In
the spring, they show
off oversized, four-
petaled, gleaming white
flowers; in the fall, bright
red berries sit above
blazing red-purple leaves.
Just above the falls, large
cedar trees dot the hillside.
Each tree has an old scar on
the same side, probably
caused by fires that swept
through here in the early 1900s
after the area was logged for its
lofty white and red pine.

Several worn paths lead out to
rocks overlooking the river along
the next section of trail. As you hike
up and down riverside ravines, the
sounds of falling water are never far
away and, during high water, constant.
Follow them and you can find paths to
most of the falls.

Watch the right side of the trail as it
passes near the river. You'll see two rock
pinnacles jut up along the trail on the
riverside. These 30- and 35-foot-tall
towers mark the deepening of the river
gorge. A few hundred feet beyond the towers you can hike up onto a
large quarter-acre rock face that gives you a splendid view of the gorge
and your first glimpse back at Lake Superior. Be careful because the
60- to 100-foot drop from the edge of the rock face is sheer and
unguarded. Also, some of the rock top you're walking on is frost shattered, and pieces can break underfoot and throw you off balance.

You can access the main trail again from the upstream end of the
rock top. The trail passes a campsite on the left, then descends into
and around a bend in a deep ravine. Stay close to the river bank until
you come to some concrete footings, which are the only remaining

Legend

Parking	P
Trail	—
Intersecting Trail	
Bridge	
Off-Trail Route	××××
Shelter	⊓
View	

evidence of a bridge that was swept away when an ice jam broke up in April 1997.

Before you get to the new bridge a little farther upstream, note the nearby campsite and check out the comment book sheltered in a wood box. Many of the comments are fascinating, for example, "Robert and Marie, 9/14, Great Sex on a Great Trail." Who says hiking doesn't have sex appeal?

Just before you reach the new bridge, just downhill from the campsite, note the large spruce stump on the hillside on the right. The stump is about 20 inches in diameter, and its growth rings indicate that it was about 70 years old when it was cut—to build the bridge you're about to cross. Its trunk forms the support that spans the river and on which the planks are fastened. Cross the bridge and check out the muck near the river on the other side for animal prints. Large canine prints, perhaps wolf, are not uncommon.

The trail now traces the river on the opposite bank, as you head downstream. You'll pass the other footing of the missing bridge, then continue on for a few hundred feet until you come to a campsite sign. Don't head up the hillside to the campsite unless you want to camp, because the trail continues down the river about 50 feet to a sign declaring "Split Rock Shelter 1.5 miles."

After another quarter mile, the trail turns left and begins a gradual ascent toward your next goal, the overlook at the Split Rock Shelter. The woods become almost entirely aspen, small ones, 9 to 12 inches in diameter. The path here can be wet and mucky. Eventually the aspen give way to birch of about the same size. Shortly after you notice the change in tree types, you can begin to see the Split Rock River valley off in the distance to the right, between the trees. And then, rather suddenly and dramatically, the vast expanse of Lake Superior stretches before you. The view will quicken your pace, even if you're tired from the day's many climbs.

But there's one more climb, a 100-foot scramble of about 20 vertical feet to a windswept hilltop with short, stunted red and white pines. An Adirondack-style shelter sits at the hill's high point. There's a trail map board inside if you'd like to orient yourself. Better yet, take in the view. On a clear day, Wisconsin's Bayfield peninsula is visible, as are some of the Apostle Islands.

When it's time to leave, follow the trail around the edge of the hilltop for about 150 yards, where you'll come to a sign that says "Hwy. 61 Parking" and that points toward a right turn down a spur trail. Take the turn and stay right all the way down the hill, avoiding a cutoff to the left that would take you back up to the Superior Hiking Trail. On the spur trail, you'll walk about a half mile to the highway. Once there, you can walk along the shoulder of the road about a quarter mile back to the wayside.

2

Vermilion Falls
Superior National Forest

Distance: 1 mile, round trip

Time: 45 minutes

Path: The walking is relatively easy, up some man-made steps and then along dirt paths. You'll also hike over some massive granite ledges, common in this region. There are lots of trail signs and some railings near the falls, but be careful—a slip near the edge could mean a 30-foot fall onto some mighty hard basalt.

Directions: From the intersection of County Highway 24 and Forest Road 491, go approximately 7 miles west on FR 491 to the parking area across the Vermilion River, on the left side of the road.

Contact: Superior National Forest, LaCroix Ranger District, 320 N. Highway 53, Cook, MN 55723; (218)666-0020.

Highlights: Rivers are always fascinating, all the more so when they tumble through rocky crags and splash down big boulders. The Vermilion offers this and history: a spot where hundreds of years ago, the voyageurs, French-Canadian trappers and settlers, pitted themselves against this rugged landscape and survived, even flourished.

Vermilion Falls is located on the Vermilion River, near the end of its journey between Vermilion Lake to the south and Crane Lake, a few miles to the north. The Vermilion was an important river to the voyageurs. They would paddle their canoes packed with furs upriver (which is actually south) against the current, make the Savanna Portage, and then travel down the St. Louis River to the Grand Portage, near present-day Duluth, where they would sell or trade their furs.

Vermilion Falls also demanded a portage, one to which this hike leads. Start from the parking area by climbing up five lovely hand-crafted granite steps. As you continue an easy climb on wooden steps, then on a cement walkway, the river is on your left. Continue straight where the trail divides. (A right turn will take you to the picnic area.)

As the trail parallels the river, you can occasionally glimpse water about 35 feet below, through the trees. You'll pass a pretty little stand of bracken fern, dotted with fernlike horsetail, on the right. Finally, after mounting four more finely fashioned stone steps and a massive granite outcrop, you'll reach a bench perched on a granite ledge overlooking the river. The opposite bank is visible for several hundred yards. Pine and aspen break the horizon above the silvery river.

When you reach a sign that says "Portage" and points left, go straight ahead to see the falls, before tracing the portage route. Down the trail about 100 feet you'll see another sign, which says "Falls" and points left. After a few steps in that direction, you'll hear water crashing through the rock canyon. This is Vermilion Falls, where you'll find yourself at the top of a canyon, over an initial 10-foot drop. Walk downriver (left) until you reach a bench and a set of wood railings. This is a great spot from which to look down and up at the falls, which are really a narrow two-channeled chute through brownish-red bedrock.

Explore the area but be careful. It's fun scrambling around on the jumble of rock. Let your eyes follow the river out below the falls, beyond the last pool, where river makes a sharp left turn. The little blind bay beyond yields nice-sized smallmouth bass.

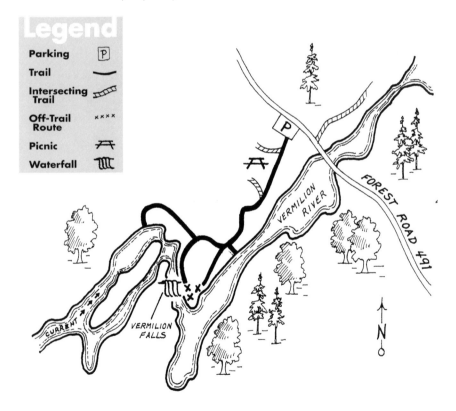

Legend

Parking	P
Trail	—
Intersecting Trail	
Off-Trail Route	x x x x
Picnic	
Waterfall	

There are no signs that take you back to the portage trail, but if you head slightly right from the base of the falls, uphill and out of sight of the river, you'll find a path that intersects another path. Turn right on that path. It's only a few hundred feet back to the river and to the beginning of the Voyageur Portage. A sign at the river's edge reads "High Falls 6 Rods." After imagining the loads the voyageurs must have carried along this route, drag yourself back up the path, past the intersection, onto a little section of trail you hiked on the way out to the falls, past the "Falls" sign, and toward the other side of the portage. Once on the new trail, you'll pass a couple of cedar posts on which modern canoeists can hang their gear. The voyageurs never had it this good.

When you reach the river again, you'll be above the falls. From this vantage point, there's no hint that there even is a falls. For as far as you can see upriver, it is placid. If you were a voyageur, you'd only have several hundred miles and 20 or 30 portages to go. Glad you're on a short hike?

Retrace your route from here back to the parking area. Your falls adventure is over.

Hidden Falls and Fawn Trails
Nerstrand Big Woods State Park

Distance: 2.5 miles

Time: 1 to 2 hours

Path: Hidden Falls Trail is over six feet wide and surfaced with hard-packed limestone gravel. Fawn Trail is about four feet wide and mostly dirt. Both are well marked and easy to follow.

Directions: From the intersection of Highways 3 and 246 in Northfield, take 246 south approximately 11 miles to Highway 40. Turn right on 40, and the park entrance is a little over 1 mile on the right.

Contact: Nerstrand Big Woods State Park, 9700 170th Street East, Nerstrand, MN 55053; (507)334-8848.

Highlights: The park preserves the state's largest remaining section of the old Bois Grand, or "Big Woods," a large, 3,000-square-mile area that was originally spread across southeast Minnesota. Although most of its woodlands were cleared by early settlers, the area still boasts of a variety of trees and plant life. Hidden Falls is a small treasure that shouldn't be missed.

Start your hike from the playground area just north of the park office, where a signboard signals the trail entrance to the woods. Also note the warning sign. It alerts you to wild parsnip, a nonnative plant that can cause skin discoloration and blistering when contacted. Read the sign and avoid the plant, along with poison ivy, which is found throughout the park.

In the next third of a mile the trail drops 140 feet, a gradual but noticeable descent. Lots of birds inhabit the area. Woodpeckers are abundant in the fall, and you may even see the uncommon redheaded woodpecker if you're lucky.

This is Minnesota's Driftless Area, unglaciated during the last Wisconsin glacial period, 10,000 years ago. But—the glacier left its mark. The deep ravine on the left is a result of glacial meltwater coursing north and east toward the torrent that was to become the Mississippi River. Off to the right, a hump of prairie rises above the landscape, and some deer trails run up onto it. Lousewort, a native plant with a fernlike leaf, grows here. You may notice its spiky yellowish flower in late spring. A young 40-foot-high stand of aspen marks the end of the prairie hump.

The trail, still descending, enters a woods full of red and white oak trees. Under them 11 species of fern prosper. The stems of the maid-enhair ferns, the ones with circular swirls of leaves, were used by Native Americans for weaving. When you reach the sign that says "Sensitive Area," you are among dwarf trout lilies. These beauties are extremely rare, growing only in three counties in Minnesota and nowhere else in the world! They sport a pale pink flower, and their average bloom time here is April 26. If you don't see them while they are in bloom, you'll likely miss them. By fall, they and most other spring ephemerals will have disappeared.

A boardwalk takes you through the forest's sensitive area, where, if it's not too late in the year, you can see an abundance of flowers: hepatica, wild ginger, and cohosh, to name a few. Just past where the boardwalk ends, marsh marigolds carpet the low area on the right in midspring. If you look left, you can see that the trail has neared a minor tributary of Prairie Creek that is soon joined by the main branch. If it's late summer or the fall, you can't miss the asparagus-like horsetail that covers the ground a little farther down the trail. Later in the hike, you'll walk through the middle of this Lilliputian forest of green stems.

When you reach a trail junction, go straight, out onto a flagstone walkway. You can hear Hidden Falls, which lies just a few yards ahead. The falls drop only about 10 feet, but the effect is impressive as the water plunges straight down the sheer rock face. It seems that this Platteville limestone bedrock fractures in straight, vertical lines, cre-ating a rather dramatic, chiseled look. You would swear that someone cut the falls into the stone.

Take the stairway down to the bottom of the falls and you can look back up at it. There's a little pool below the falls that sometimes harbors trout. Look for them jumping and rising to insects. Beyond the pond you can see pieces of limestone strewn up above the bank, which were tossed there by high water during a raging flood in June 1998.

At this point you can go back to the trail and turn right, a path that will take you across the creek on some functional, if aesthetically unattractive concrete blocks. While a bridge would make for a more eye-pleasing crossing, park personnel have found that bridges often wash out. Even the massive blocks placed in the creek have moved a bit when spring floodwaters hit them.

Across the creek, bear right at the large signboard and you'll be on the Fawn Trail. Climb past an old snag full of pileated woodpecker holes on the left and you'll reach another signboard. The trail to the left is Fawn Trail returning. Bear right. You'll then pass a deer exclosure on the left. This fenced area was constructed in order to see what happens when deer, who eat away the understory, are excluded from a particular area of the woods. This one has been compromised by a tree that has fallen across the fence, providing an opening for the deer.

The trail traces the rim of the creek valley, which is on the right, for the next quarter mile or so. Along this stretch, you'll see the least disturbed area of trees on this hike. Note some of the bigger basswood, along with white and red oak. These trees are over 100 years old and date back before the time that the woods were selectively logged. The understory

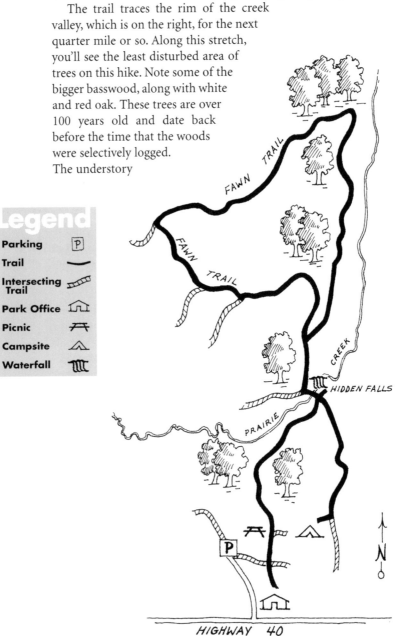

Legend

Parking	P
Trail	—
Intersecting Trail	
Park Office	
Picnic	
Campsite	
Waterfall	

FAWN TRAIL

FAWN TRAIL

CREEK

HIDDEN FALLS

PRAIRIE

P

N

HIGHWAY 40

is composed mostly of nettles, stinging native plants with fibrous stems that, like maidenhair ferns, can be used for making baskets or even nets.

You'll loop gently over a little rise and turn back left. This is a great place for wood thrushes and oven birds especially in the spring when you can hear their calls. As the trail gradually dips down into a valley, look for a change in the woods. Here, there are more low-growing plants, fewer big trees. Some of the trees are multistemmed, having sprouted from stumps after the older trees were cut.

When you reach a little creek bed, walk over to it and examine the dark, almost black, glacially derived soil that erosion has left exposed here. The soil lies on top of the same type of limestone that you saw at the falls.

At a trail junction just after you reach the creek bed, a sign says "Fawn Trail and Hidden Falls" with an arrow pointing left. Take this trail and you'll climb briefly through even denser undergrowth, where lots of seedling trees thrive, the beginnings of the next generation's woodland.

Turn left at the next junction and you'll loop down and rejoin the trail not far from Hidden Falls. Retrace this trail to the falls and then rejoin the Hidden Falls Trail, where you then move through the stand of horsetail that you saw on the hike out. There is a small stand of large red oak on the left as you climb the 140 feet that you descended walking down to the falls. Then the trail breaks into a clearing, and you'll see a farm and field on the left. Bear right at the next junction and you'll exit the trail at campsite number 18. Go left on the camp road; it's a short walk back to the visitor center and park office.

In the Footsteps of the Voyageurs

4
Vermilion Gorge
Superior National Forest

Distance: 3 miles

Time: 1.5 hours

Path: The surface is gravel for the first half of the hike, then it becomes an amalgam of dirt, rocks, and roots. There are some steep and long hills on both parts of the hike. The last part of the hike is not recommended because of its difficult and dangerous traverse of a precipitous hillside, just reported.

Directions: Take Highway 24 north from its intersection with Highway 23 in Buyck until the road ends near the Voyageurs National Park office, a distance of about 14 miles. The trailhead is a short walk past the office on the left.

Contact: Superior National Forest, LaCroix Ranger District, 320 N. Highway 53, Cook, MN 55723; (218)666-0020.

Highlights: Make no mistake about it—this hike is a challenge. The hills are tough and the path rough. But you'll be rewarded with views of a wonderfully wild and historic river.

B egin this hike from the parking area next to the trailhead, where a signboard announces the start of the trail. Be ready for a steep climb that lasts for several minutes. About halfway up the hill on the left, three big white pine dominate the scene. Each is over 30 inches in diameter and qualify as old growth. But the most impressive pine is a recently deceased specimen on the right. It's the biggest of the three, over 3 feet in diameter, and likely the tallest. It's not clear what killed it, but a good guess is that lightning struck it, perhaps several times, many years ago, and that it survived the effects until only recently.

Near the top of the hill, the hiking trail turns right and a snowmobile trail goes off to the left. There is a signboard that describes Rene Bourassa's 1736 trading post. This earliest of outposts was a center of contact between the French explorers and the native population. The trail eventually takes you near its location on the Vermilion River.

Twenty-one steps take you back downhill again, the first of many ups and downs along the trail. You'll tread a boardwalk that spans a low area full of basswood, aspen, and spruce, with large-leafed aster and hazelnut being the predominant understory. Along the trail, some large red pine are mixed with the others, with the first about halfway up the next hill. A series of steps made from railroad ties takes you down yet another hill, around a bend, and under a tipped-over aspen.

At the start of another boardwalk, which spans a small, sometimes dry creek bed, you'll encounter your first white cedar. Beyond the creek is an expanse of forest that's been obviously wracked by a ferocious wind. Aspen stand topless and branchless, with their branches having been ripped off in what must have been a mighty storm. Other trees have been blown over, their roots ripped out of the ground. The result is an open forest where abundant sunlight hits the ground and new trees, shrubs, and groundcover emerge. It's a dense, brushy place.

The trail soon reaches the Vermilion River for the first time. The river is wide, like the St. Croix at Taylors Falls, or the Mississippi above St. Paul. This is where the Vermilion empties itself into Crane Lake and near where Rene Bourassa built his trading post. A signboard next to the river tells about the post and how the Indians traded furs to the voyageurs for guns, metal pots, and knives. In the spring, the

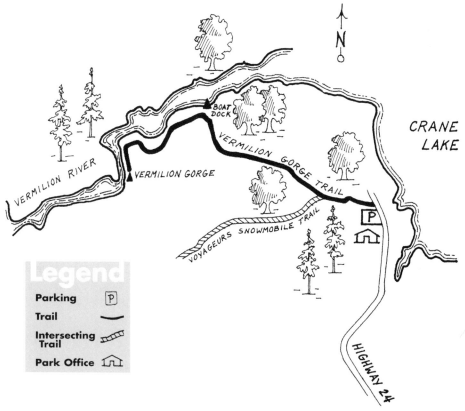

voyageurs carried the furs up the river through the Savanna Portage and down the St. Louis River to the Grand Portage, where they sold or traded them.

From this point on, the hike becomes more difficult because the trail is less even. The hills are steeper too, like the one that awaits just beyond. You'll climb more than 60 vertical feet in fewer than 100 feet of distance, a challenge typical of several more you'll encounter before reaching the gorge. A set of wooden steps takes you up another 15 feet or so, and you can see the river through the trees about 75 feet below. The trees here are mostly smaller red pine, precariously rooted in thin soil atop massive bedrock outcrops. You'll hike over a lot of this rock in the next half mile. The trail is canted at many different angles, sometimes making for an easy, flat footfall, sometimes for a difficult, ankle-twisting ordeal.

The trail makes a close approach to the river and to a wooden dock provided by the Forest Service for boaters who want to hike to the gorge. It's only a brief scramble over some rocks and roots until you reach the beginning of the gorge, where you'll hear the sounds of rushing water before you see it. The trail breaks into several smaller ones here, which many hikers have used as shortcuts to reach the edge of the bank overlooking the gorge. Resist following these side trails and instead head upstream a few hundred feet to where the trail has been improved with wood planks. You'll see the gorge. It's narrow, perhaps only 7 or 8 feet wide in places and about 80 feet deep. The rock walls are naked, swept of any vegetation by violent currents. Near the top, above the waterline, polypody ferns manage to populate the crevices. If you look upstream, you can see the beginning of the gorge and, above it, a tranquil flat-water river. Beyond is a 90-degree bend in the river.

The trail really ends here, but there is a goat path along the edge of a steep, sandy, highly erodible bank. The path is less than a foot wide in places, and there's a good chance of slipping and falling 30 or 40 feet into the rocky river below. The goat trail ends near the bottom of the bank, from where you can see upriver, past the 90-degree bend, for a half mile or so. The river here is wide and placid, probably not worth the risk involved in getting to where you can see it.

When you've seen enough, turn around and retrace your steps along the same trail. You'll be impressed at how long and steep the former downhill pitches have become now that they are uphill.

Grand Portage Trail
Jay Cooke State Park

Distance: 3 miles

Time: 1.5 to 2 hours

Path: The first half of this hike is not easy. The path is narrow, mostly uphill, and sometimes slippery because of wet mud. There are rocks and some roots, with uneven footing being the norm. However, it is well marked, and so you should not have any trouble staying on the trail.

Directions: From the intersection of I-35 and Highway 210 south of Cloquet, take 210 approximately 6 miles east to the park entrance. Continue on 210 for 3 miles to the park headquarters and picnic area, which are on the right. Continue for an additional 3 miles until you see a parking area on the right.

Contact: Jay Cooke State Park, 500 East Highway 210, Carlton, MN 55718; (218)384-4610.

Highlights: Lovely river views and a wonderful woodland on this hike, which traces the trail of the voyageurs.

This hike starts at the St. Louis River. To get there, park in the lot off Highway 210 and hike away from the river, following an electric power line along an old railroad bed. In 100 yards or so you'll reach a large sign that proclaims this the Grand Portage and describes some of the backbreaking efforts made by the people who traveled it. Turn right at the sign and walk another 100 yards or so to the river. Large slabs of basalt, old lava flows, jut out into the river here. This is where hundreds, perhaps thousands, of portages started, dating back to prehistoric times, when Native Americans hauled their canoes and other possessions onto the shore.

From the river, retrace your path to the big sign and then continue across the railroad grade, up a small embankment; in a few hundred feet you'll cross Highway 210. Head back into the woods and begin a long uphill trudge through a dense deciduous forest. Your legs and lungs will get a brief respite as the trail levels out and hugs the hillside, then it heads uphill again, repeating this undulating pattern a couple of times. At the edge of the trail, you'll walk past an enormous white spruce, a giant, with a three-foot diameter, that no doubt witnessed some of the later portages along this route.

The trail makes another dip and crosses some wet terrain, with slippery rocks and all. The path climbs again, this time into a coniferous woods, with some tall, straight white pine. A deep ravine drops precipitously to the left, and tall pine and spruce are visible on the opposite side. After crossing another dip and more slippery rock, you can hear the sound of running water off to the left in the ravine. As the trail loops back almost 180 degrees and descends into the ravine, you'll reach a narrow stream that has no bridge. As you cross the water, imagine carrying a canoe, not a 40-pound Kevlar wonder but a 200-pound voyageur birch-bark, circa 1700. Imagine also carrying several 75-pound packs in relays up and down the hills you've crossed. We can't be sure of the kind of vegetation the early travelers had to trudge through here, but it was probably a lot like the present-day stuff. We can be sure, however, that there were mosquitos, flies, and other vermin making the portage miserable.

Experts tell us that the voyageurs and others headed downhill from here, back near the St. Louis River. The hiking trail that you are following departs from the old portage trail and continues uphill. The present-day trail will rejoin the portage trail at the top of the hill and end by tracing the portage trail downstream.

After crossing the stream, the trail climbs steeply and enters a younger woods, without many conifers. There are lots of alder, which is a wetland shrub or sometimes a tree. It is odd finding them after a long, steep climb, but they are a sign that your climb isn't over yet; you are merely on a small hillside plateau. The trail continues upward, bordered by thousands of bracken and interrupted ferns. As the woods gets thinner, the trail intersects with another, one that skims the top of a moraine. Turn left at this intersection and take a good look at the deep valley on the right. The topography drops off to the left also, and you'll walk along this ridge until you reach a map board and a post numbered 24.

Loop left for about 250 yards along the Oak Trail, until you reach a large signboard that proclaims the "Fourth Pause" of the voyageurs, which is located at the top of what is called the Big Hill. Since you are tracing the voyageurs' course downriver from here, it will be a long downhill trek for you. The woods on the downhill segment are an open aspen-oak savanna. It looks as if the area may have burned 30 years ago in a fire.

Highway 210 will suddenly reappear; it has traveled in the same direction as you have since you started the hike. Cross the road and you'll be near the St. Louis again. Hike through a grove of white pine and you'll reach Roche Galet, or Shingle Rock, named by the voyageurs for the large, flat sandstone that once jutted out of the river.

It's not visible today because the dam downriver has caused the water level to rise. This rock served portagers as the spot for their "Third Pause."

From here it's about a half mile back to the parking area where you started the hike. About half the distance is along the river, with some clear views of the steep, sometimes eroded hillside on the other bank; the other half is under a power line. Watch for poison ivy here. When the trail joins Highway 210 and crosses a wet area (actually the outlet of Little River), you are only 100 yards or so from the parking area and the end of a brief glimpse into what the hardy voyageurs faced hundreds of years ago.

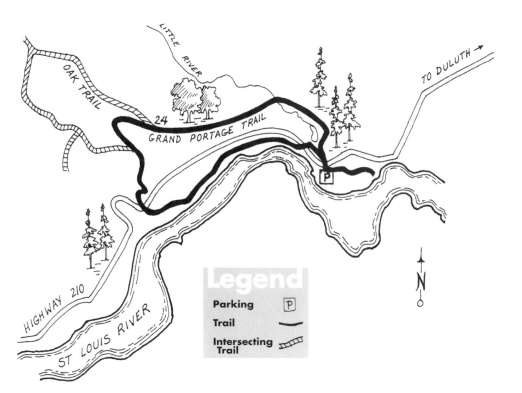

6

Savanna Portage Trail
Savanna Portage State Park

Distance: 11 miles, round trip

Time: 4 to 5 hours

Path: The first couple of miles are on often-used park trails, which are also part of a winter ski trail system. These trails are wide and mowed and generally smooth, free of roots and rocks. The next few miles are on a narrower, less smooth, and more difficult path that winds its way up and down several hills. The last mile or so may be wet, as the trail crosses an area known as the Mass of Mire. Wooden boards have been laid down so you don't sink into the mire, a problem the voyageurs no doubt faced when they traveled through the area. The early part of the Portage Trail is marked but can be confusing because of many other intersecting trails. Once out on main portion of the trail, you'll find that there's no choice but to follow it.

Directions: From the intersection of Highway 210 and Highway 65 at McGregor, take 65 north to County Highway 14. Follow 14 about 10 miles to the park entrance.

Contact: Savanna Portage State Park, HCR 3, Box 591, McGregor, MN 55760; (218)426-3271.

Highlights: Tracing the arduous path of the early explorers and encountering some of the difficult conditions they lived with.

Early explorer and geologist J. G. Norwood said that the "Savanna Portage is the worst carrying place in the Northwest." While it's a much better hiking place these days, it's nonetheless a formidable undertaking. During much of the summer, mosquitos make life difficult if you're not wearing long pants and a long sleeve shirt and packing plenty of repellent. In fact, according to a study done in 1994, there are 32 mosquito species in Savanna Portage State Park, more than anywhere else in North America except Isle Royale, Michigan.

If this doesn't scare you off, start your hike from the parking area at the historic site, a little more than a half mile into the park. And you can warm up with an easy jaunt down to the west end of this historic portage. To do so, walk just behind the historical marker and signboard to where the trail dips immediately down into the river lowland. It's only about 100 yards to a bend in the West Savanna River where the voyageurs, after a very disagreeable portage of 6 miles, must have happily relaunched their canoes on their way to the Mississippi.

Retrace your steps to the parking area and cross the road. You will see the 200-yard-long boardwalk stretching out into a sea of tall wetland grass. A sign there tells you that the Dakotas were the first recorded users of this portage. They called it "Mushkigoniqumi," or mush portage.

Once off the walkway, you'll hike though an aspen woods. Make a left turn at the first junction and then carefully follow the signs that say "Portage Trail." There are several intersections along the way that can be confusing. At a five-way intersection, called "Spaghetti Junction" by park personnel, you'll see the Continental Divide Trail off to the left. Since you began at the parking lot, you've been walking gradually uphill; now you are about to start downhill, crossing the Continental Divide that separates the Mississippi watershed from that of the Great Lakes.

Head out on the Portage Trail, through a deciduous woods with some occasional white pine. You'll pass one old white pine riddled with elongated, almost rectangular holes made by the pileated woodpecker. Note the occasional massive red oak, some with diameters as large as 28 inches, before you dip down into a wet

Legend

Parking	P
Trail	—
Intersecting Trail	⊐⊐⊐
Bridge Route	≋
Shelter	⊓
Park Office	⌂

area that harbors some white cedar. You'll soon leave the pine over-story and find more and more plank walks over wet lowlands. As you dip up and down across glacial deposits, you can see that the ground is worn quite deeply, three or four inches in some places. You are walking in the footsteps of hundreds of early explorers like Father Jacques Marquette, who traversed this portage in 1669, one of the first white men to do so. The French explorer Duluth passed through here in 1679, and Henry Schoolcraft, on his way to find the source of the Mississippi, around 1830.

After about a mile of walking you'll reach an Adirondack-style shelter located in an upland hardwood stand and near a snowmobile trail. Past the snowmobile trail the terrain becomes wet again, but you'll avoid the muck by walking along a walkway made from a couple of 2 x 10 wooden boards. You'll soon reach an old drainage ditch, dug more than 80 years ago in a futile effort at draining the area for agriculture. The trail hugs the ditch bank for awhile, then crosses the ditch on a bridge and follows the opposite bank. A sign will indicate when you reenter the Portage Trail and leave the ditch bank.

The last several hundred yards of your hike will be through cattail marsh. The trail ends at the East Savanna River, although it may not look very riverlike. Take a minute to reflect on the difficulty of this hike—then contemplate what it must have been like for the voyageurs carrying hundreds of pounds of gear and a heavy canoe!

Among Tall Trees

7

Big Aspen Trail
Superior National Forest

Distance: 1 mile

Time: 30 minutes to 1 hour

Path: Some grass, but mostly pine needles. There are some rocks and roots, but nothing taxing. The terrain is largely flat. The trail marking is good and, given the short distance involved, it would be difficult to get lost.

Directions: From Virginia, take Highway 53 north for 8 miles to County Road 131. Go right on 131 for 1 mile, then turn left on County Road 68 and proceed .3 mile to County Road 405. The parking area is located 2 miles down 405 on the left.

Contact: Superior National Forest, Laurentian Ranger District, 318 Forestry Road, Aurora, MN 55705; (218) 229-3371.

Highlights: Big old red pine mix easily with jack pine and aspen on this needle- and moss-carpeted stroll.

If ever a trail was misnamed, it's this one. Actually, there are over 20 miles of trails in this system, and this hike takes in only about a mile, so maybe somewhere there are big aspen. What we have here are big pine.

Begin your hike across the road from the parking area, just below or south of where County Road 405 splits and becomes Forest Roads 257 and 256. A 50-yard-long spur trail connects with a loop, which is just under a mile long. Take the spur trail and turn right when you reach an intersection.

There are a number of wondrous sights on this walk, and one of the first you'll notice are pine cones—hundreds, thousands, millions of them strewn across the ground. You could gather bushels full in minutes. Most of the cones have been cast off by the predominant tree here, the red, or Norway, pine. Although called Norway, these pines with reddish bark are native to this country. You'll also see cones from two other native pines, white and jack. White pine cones are the longest cones, jack pine the shortest. Jack pine don't usually shed their cones, preferring to keep them, even on branches that are long dead. That's because many of the cones don't open up and spread their seed until heated to over 100 degrees, an event that doesn't usually occur except during a fire. Better to be high in the air when this happens then lying on the ground. Squirrels often clip off jack pine cones, along with the branch tip, while feeding; you'll see much of this activity, especially late in the summer and in the fall.

Another fascinating trail sight is the moss that grows on the trail itself. One wonders how this fuzzy green carpet survives—the moss grows on the dark, damp forest floor and then gets trampled by all manner of creatures, human and otherwise. If that weren't enough, it spends half a year buried under a blanket of snow. As you proceed down this comfortable trail, look for big-leaf aster, which also carpets the forest floor in many places.

If it's a windy day, make sure you stop and listen to the wind rustle through the pines. The sound can come from anywhere above you, as the wind sneaks through the branches. There's something mystical about pines and wind and there's no better place for that mysticism than here.

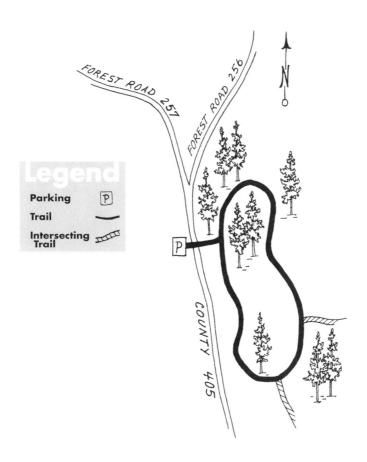

Also up in the branches, less ethereal than the wind but no less inspiring, are hosts of birds. You may not see them and you'll only hear the noisy ones, the jays and crows, but if you look down you'll see evidence of their presence. Round white dots of various sizes mark the ground. Most visible on rocks, these dots are droppings from birds.

The trail comes to a junction, which is numbered 3 on the map board. Bear left and stay on the loop. You'll soon come to some big red pine, over 20 inches in diameter, scattered along the trail. At an average of a quarter of an inch of diameter growth a year, these trees are 160 years old.

At the next junction, only a couple of hundred yards farther, bear left again. Here the trail enters an area forested with aspen and other leaf-losing trees. Also notice the clover that carpets the trail here and elsewhere. This has been planted and is a favorite food of ruffed grouse.

In wetter spots along the trail here you can see various fungi erupting from the earth. Mushrooms and toadstools are locally abundant and ephemeral, fading away within days. They play an important part in recycling the organic matter that falls to the forest floor, breaking it down into various components.

As you round the last loop on your way back to the beginning of this walk, look out for wind-blown trees across the trail. Both aspen and jack pine have shallow roots and can topple over easily in a big wind. When you reach the spur trail that brought you here, turn right and head back to the parking lot.

8

Lost Forty Trail
Chippewa National Forest

Distance: 1.5 miles

Time: 1 hour

Path: A well-worn pine needle-carpeted tread that is almost flat, save for a couple of dips and the short hill down to the brook.

Directions: From Highway 71 in Blackduck, take Highway 30/13 east to the junction with Highway 46 in Alvwood. Go north (left) on 46 for .5 mile to Highway 29; go east (right) on 29 about 11 miles to Highway 26 in Dora Lake. Take 26 north (left)for about 2 miles to Forest Road 2240. Go west (left) on 2240 about 1.5 miles to the Lost Forty parking area on the left.

Contact: Chippewa National Forest, Blackduck District, HC3–Box 95, Blackduck, MN 56630; (218)835-4291.

Highlights: Wonderful big old pines, both white and red, are the highlight of this easy walk. This is what millions of acres of Minnesota forest looked like before they were cut down.

Not many pine trees were overlooked by loggers in Minnesota back around the turn of the century. This hike takes you through acres of forest that, luckily, was overlooked. It seems that in the late 1800s Josiah King and his three-man survey team mistakenly plotted Coddington Lake a half mile north and west of its actual location. Years later, the loggers, who relied on the survey work, looked at the map and saw a lake instead of the 144-acre plot of land. They never checked closely enough to catch the error, and it wasn't found until after the loggers had swept through. Thank goodness. What we are left with today is one of the very few multiple-acre stands of big white and red pine in the lake region.

The trail begins just across Forest Road 2240 from the parking area. As you cross the road, note the outsized red pine log lying along the road. His roots show that this fellow must have toppled over in a windstorm. The top has been cut off so that the limbs don't block the road. The remaining trunk is about 35 feet long, and the cut across the top is 22 inches in diameter, meaning that this giant was almost 2 feet across, 35 feet in the air. A lot of yard trees have only thin branches and leaves that high in the air!

There's a signboard and pamphlet box at the trailhead. If you're lucky enough to get a pamphlet, it provides a rudimentary map of the short trail and brief descriptions of what you'll find at numbered posts along the way, with occasional references to the post numbers.

As you begin down the trail, notice the double-layered forest. Underneath the towering pines are smaller trees, most of them shade-tolerant maples but also some aspen, birch, and others. These trees would comprise the entire forest canopy in most woodlands but here they are only the bottom tree layer in a canopy over 100 feet high.

After post number 2, you'll see another fallen red pine. Note its modest root system and also that it's very close to the much-trodden path. There's little doubt that years of footsteps have compacted the soil and injured the roots on the path side, predisposing the tree to wind throw.

At post number 3, the stand of enormous trees ends, and you enter an area that was cut over in the late 1800s and then burned in the early 1900s. But a lot of red pine still survive, most of them straight and tall, with diameters of around 24 inches. Notice the reddish tinge to their bark. This is what gives them their common name—red pine. Another common name is Norway pine, although these pine are native to the lake states and not from Norway. Their scientific name is *Pinus resinosa*.

As you continue your walk, you'll notice that many of the red pine have inverted V-shaped indentations at their bases. These are old fire scars. When ground fires sweep through red pine, they may cause some damage to the trees, but the mature ones, because of their thick bark, usually survive and continue to grow. These scars are the result of the healing process in which new live tissue (cambium) grows out and around the fire wound, thus walling off fungus and other rots. As a matter of fact, a healthy tree does this with any wound.

After a couple of ups and downs, the trail reaches a junction. If you continue on straight, you'll hike though an even younger woods that was logged in the 1940s. Much more recently, a wind storm knocked down most of the balsam fir and some other trees. The shattered nature of the breaks in their trunks suggests a sustained high wind, with some gusting.

When you reach the short, steep downgrade to Moose Brook, hike on down to see if you can spot a moose. Although the area has a moose population, you're more likely to see some waterfowl or other bird life.

Head back to the junction with the loop trail leading from the parking area and go right. At post number 9, you can see another fallen red pine. The cut has exposed approximately 175 rings, an indication that the tree was probably 175 years old when it was felled. A glance to the right, however, reveals that there is at least 30 feet of tree trunk below the cut. So the tree was older than 175 years—perhaps 30, perhaps 100 years older.

As you finish this walk, you'll no doubt be awed by the age of these magnificent trees and perhaps be a bit saddened that there are not more like them. When white settlers first arrived in Minnesota, there were several million acres of such old growth forest. Today there are less than 25,000 acres in the state, and they are fragmented. You have just hiked one of the bigger such tracts.

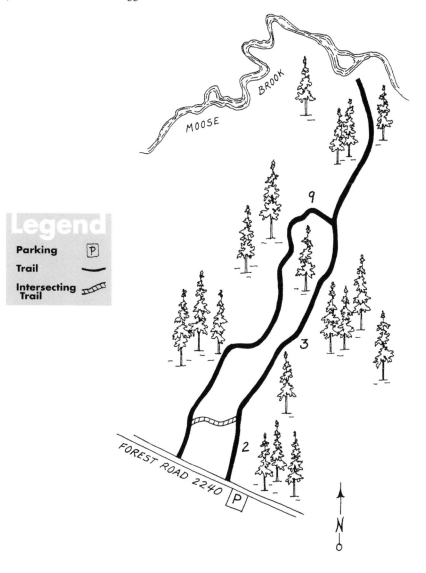

Legend

Parking   P

Trail   —

Intersecting Trail

Mississippi Headwaters and Schoolcraft Trails
Itasca State Park

Distance: 3 miles

Time: 1.5 hours

Path: Worn dirt in some places, mowed grass in others. Since this hike puts together a couple of routes, the paths differ a bit. The trails are easy to follow and pretty flat. The surface is fairly even without lots of rocks and roots. This is an easy walk.

Directions: From Park Rapids, take Highway 71 north about 20 miles to County Highway 122. Turn north on 122 (left) into the park. Stay on the road for about 7 miles and enjoy the wonderful old-growth pines amid many little lakes. You'll also pass historic Douglas Lodge, the park campground office, the entrance to the University of Minnesota Forestry and Biological Station, the park headquarters, and other facilities on your way to the museum parking area.

Contact: Itasca State Park, HC05, Box 4, Lake Itasca, MN 56360; (218)266-2114.

Highlights: This is a walk to the headwaters of the longest river in the United States and one of the longest in the world. It also takes you out along the headwaters lake for a look at an island named after the man who is credited with discovering the headwaters.

The museum where you begin this walk is well worth a visit, if for no other reason than to see the exhibit on Henry Schoolcraft, the explorer who discovered the headwaters of the Mississippi in 1832. There had been many explorers who claimed to have found the headwaters before Schoolcraft, but they had all been mistaken about the actual location. Even the famous Jean Nicolet had been wrong, although he was the closest, choosing (and naming) Nicolet Creek at the north end of Lake Itasca's west arm as the headwaters. Schoolcraft relied on Ozawindib, leader of the Anishinabe, to assist him in finding the beginning of the mighty Mississippi. There are lots of other excellent exhibits in the museum, so give yourself enough time to check them out.

After leaving the museum, turn left onto a dirt path along the lake that winds through a parklike picnic area. You'll cross a wooden bridge that spans a gulch, then pass a log restroom. You'll soon see the "Headwaters 800 feet" sign and perhaps your pace will quicken.

When you reach the opening that marks the headwaters, you can see a span of boulders, some as large as basketballs and even truck tires, that create a gentle arc across the water. On one side of the arc is Lake Itasca, stretching out in the distance to the far shore. On the other side of the rock arc is the Mississippi, here only a narrow, weakly flowing stream but nonetheless a beginning. Walk across the rocks but be careful. They have been trodden so much that they have been polished smooth and are very slippery.

Actually, the rocks are a modern addition. They sit atop a concrete dam that, along with 2,000 loads of sand and gravel, was set here in 1933 by the Civilian Conservation Corps. It seems that the park superintendent at the time didn't feel that the headwaters were dramatic enough, with the river quietly beginning in a cattail marsh at the north end of Lake Itasca. So he authorized the "improvement."

As you continue your walk, now alongside the Mississippi River, you'll reach a bridge over the river, the first of an almost uncountable number of bridges between here and the river's delta south of New Orleans. From the bridge, look upriver toward the lake. You'll see cattail and other marsh plants. There is a discernable difference in the texture and types of plants growing straight toward the lake. These mark the old channel. The view gives you a reasonable snapshot of what Henry Schoolcraft and Ozawindib saw back in 1832.

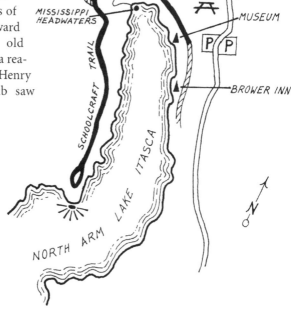

Legend

Parking	P
Trail	—
Intersecting Trail	⊐⊐⊐
Bridge	≋
Picnic	⊼
View	☀

While still on the bridge, turn and look downriver. Think about where this river is going: It will drop 1,475 feet before reaching sea level, about half of which will be before it leaves Minnesota, and it will travel 2,552 miles.

When you're ready, continue across the bridge and down a boardwalk to a trail junction. A right turn will take you to the visitor center and parking lot for the headwaters area. The center provides additional information about the Mississippi and other rivers of the world that was not in the museum. It's worth a visit.

Continuing on, you keep left, down the Schoolcraft Trail. One of the first things you'll notice is that many of the tree trunks are blackened by fire, the result of a "prescribed burn" started by park personnel. The idea is to reproduce conditions that favor the germination of pine seeds, which need mineral-rich soil, and reduced competition from shrubs and understory plants. The process is still experimental, and some biologists disagree about this treatment, if for no other reason than the fires sometimes get out of control. (See the Blind Ash Bay Trail walk for a description of one such burn.)

The next unusual sight along the trail is a fallen red pine, its twisted, spiraling limbs lying in a heap on the ground, with brown moplike needle clusters drooping from the ends of its branches. Its top, which blocks the trail, is cut off, and even 30 feet above its base the tree is over 2 feet in diameter.

As the trail loops back near Lake Itasca, you can see the park beach and bathhouse across on the opposite shore. Then you head inland again, eventually reaching a junction created by a trail loop. Bear right, through a raspberry thicket, past another big fallen red pine, a vast tamarack bog on the right, and near some large, 32-inch-diameter white spruce on the left.

Suddenly you'll come upon basswood trees and the woods seem to change character. You have reached Hill Point. Visit the bench by the signboard and gaze out across the lake to Schoolcraft Island, where Henry Schoolcraft camped with his Anishinabe guides. This is an historic view.

Head back past the Indian cemetery, which occupies a prominent spot out on this lovely point. You'll see more downed trees along here than on most other sections of the trail, because they are exposed to harsher conditions and stronger winds from the lake. One fallen spruce that had blocked the trail has been cut, its growth rings indicating that it was at least 120 years when it fell.

Soon afterwards, you'll reach the junction where you'll rejoin the trail segment that brought you out here. Bear right and you'll retrace your steps back to the headwaters area. If you like, visit the headwaters display area or loop back around the top of the lake to the museum.

The Learning Trail
Robert E. Ney Memorial Park

Distance: 3 miles

Time: 1.5 hours

Path: This path has a variety of surfaces. It starts out as chipped wood, then becomes dirt, then mowed grass. It's hilly and well marked, but since there are several multipath junctions, it can be tricky; pay attention.

Directions: From the intersection of Highway 55 and County Road 8 in Maple Lake, take 8 north 1.5 miles to the sign for the park. Turn right on this road and follow the signs to the parking area; it's about .5 mile on the left.

Contact: Wright County Parks, 1901 Highway 25 North, Buffalo, MN 55313; (612)682-7693 or (800)362-3667, extension 7693.

Highlights: This walk is through a diverse habitat, with big hardwood trees and lush wetlands.

Start your hike from beside the nature center, just up the asphalt walkway from the parking area. There are lots of hills along this trail, and you'll trudge up one immediately. There's a bench at the top that affords you a great view of Lake Mary.

Make your way downhill to a junction and go left. The trail traces the base of the hill you just traversed, looping back downhill of the nature center, which is visible above. There's a very large ironwood tree on the left as you pass the nature center.

Turn right at the next junction, which is a four-pronged affair just past a little creek bed and a large wet meadow. You'll see a box elder tree bent over the trail, greeting you with a graceful arch. On the right is a scruffy little stand of balsam fir, an evergreen that smells wonderful when its needles are crushed.

Continuing down the trail, you'll pass through a lowland, with a long, sloping hillside on the left. Here large black ash hold sway, along with some tall, clear-stemmed silver maple. Just on the edge of the trail where it bends right, you'll see another notable tree, an American elm with a 16-inch diameter. Large elms like this one are rare these days after Dutch elm disease devastated the nation's elm population in the 1950s and 1960s.

The trail then climbs up and out of the lowland. Along the way, check out the bench that affords a view of bottomland to the east. You'll also note that the woods have changed. Gone are the bigger trees, and what's left are smaller trees and brush.

When you reach the next junction, turn right. Just beyond your turning point, you'll see trail marker 11, which marks a red-twig dogwood. But you may want to pay more attention to what's next to it, a 15-foot-tall buckthorn tree, which is an unusually large specimen. Its 3-inch diameter single stem displays exfoliating bark, rather like a yellow birch tree. Buckthorn is an unwelcome nonnative plant, usu-

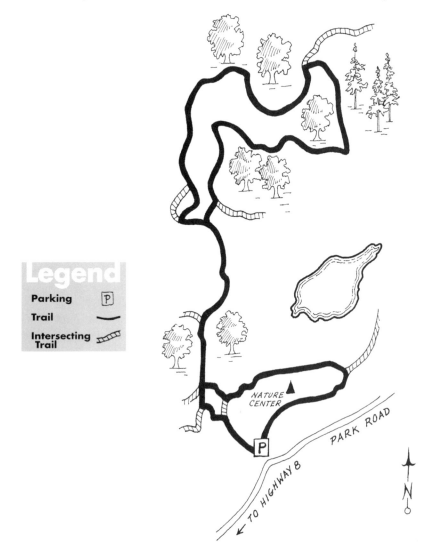

Legend

Parking   P

Trail

Intersecting Trail

NATURE CENTER

P

TO HIGHWAY 8

PARK ROAD

N

ally a shrub, that overwhelms other native woodland vegetation. This is an unusually large specimen.

It's not far to the next junction, where you'll want to bear left and climb a long, gently sloping hill. There's a large, wind-shattered red oak trunk sticking 25 feet into the air on the right, one of the many broken trees along this section of trail. A tornado in July 1997 left a mess that took the park's personnel weeks to clean up.

Once you've passed the wind-damaged area, you'll stroll through a forest with trees of various ages. Venerable old red oak, basswood, and sugar maple lift their big limbs, canted at odd angles, above and through smaller butternut, hickory, basswood, sugar maple, and oak. Eventually, the trail enters a red pine plantation, with sumac and elm filling every little opening not occupied by the pine. Given the wonderful performance of hardwoods here, one wonders why anyone would plant red pine.

After a sweeping downhill trek, go left at the next junction and you'll pass through a clearing and back into a deciduous woods. You'll see a two-acre pothole on the right, its light green, wetland vegetation contrasting with the surrounding woods. You'll pass through another area where trees have been ripped apart by the tornado. A ripped-off red oak top is visible on the left. A reading of its rings shows that it was 97 years old when it was felled by the storm, and this reading is at a point on the tree that would have been 25 to 30 feet off the ground.

When you reach the next junction, continue straight ahead, up a steep 20-yard climb. There's a bench at the top, but trees have obscured the view. At the next junction, only 100 yards ahead, turn left and you'll reach another junction, near where the red-twig dogwood and big-stemmed buckthorn are located. Bear right and you'll be back on the trail that brought you here.

When you reach the four-pronged junction, just past the arching box elder, continue straight to the next junction where you should go left and cross a little bridge. Note the lush wetland on the right and the road beyond. Keep to the right, past several clumps of lovely river birch, a tree near its northernmost extent here. In a few yards you'll be in a picnic area near the parking lot, which is just ahead. Check out the Robert E. Ney Memorial Chapel on the left. In 1970, Albert Ney dedicated the land you have just hiked as a nature preserve to honor his son, Robert, who was killed in World War II. We are all richer for Albert's gift.

Bogs, Marshes, and Wetlands

Orr Area Bog Walk
Voyageurs National Park

Distance: .5 mile

Time: 45 minutes

Path: The entire walk is on a pierlike boardwalk above the fragile bog. There are interpretive signs along the way. For those who worry about getting lost in the woods, this walk is for you. There's no way you can stray off this path without getting mighty wet!

Directions: The walk is located in Voyageurs National Park; the Orr Area Information Center is on the west side of Highway 53 just south of the village of Orr.

Contact: Voyageurs National Park and Orr Area Information Center, P.O. Box 236, Orr, MN 55771; (800)357-9255.

Highlights: This man-made path is a wonder in itself. If you've ever slogged through a bog, you'll appreciate the effort that went into its construction. The wetland communities represented here are wonderful, unique, and difficult to access anywhere else. Intelligent trailside signs teach you about the area's vegetation.

Start this walk in the southwest corner of the parking area. A couple of fine highbush cranberry bushes adorn the entrance to the walkway, holding high, flat-topped, multiblossomed cymes of white flowers in early summer, and bright-red pea-sized fruit all clustered together, in the fall and winter.

Upon entering the boardwalk, you'll immediately be walking under a canopy of large black ash trees. These compound-leafed trees love wet sites. This is technically a black ash swamp, not a bog, the distinction being the degree of wetness and the resulting plants that grow in each type of ecosystem. Notice that there are only a few types of plants growing here under the ash. Horsetail love it, as evidenced by the vast numbers of them. Currants like it here too, their maple-shaped leaves waving in the breeze up to 4 feet above the ground. In the spring you may see some purple-fringed orchids or marsh marigolds.

When the boardwalk splits into two branches, take the right one. Shortly afterwards, you'll begin seeing tamarack. Also called larch, these are the only coniferous trees (producing seeds via cone production) that lose all their needles in the fall. The needles turn a lovely golden color before they drop, often after most other trees have lost their leaves. As you move through the tamarack, notice the two on the left that have tipped over. By falling over, they have exposed their root systems to close-up inspection since they are only a foot from the boardwalk. The mass of intertwined roots from the two trees measure about 14 by 20 feet across. Notice how there are no deep or tap roots. Trees that grow in very wet places must keep their "feet" as dry as possible, and boring them deep into the earth is not the solution. Roots that spread out across the top of the bog provide a better platform and one that other plants can use too.

As you walk along, alder gradually will replace the tamarack. At first there will only be a few alder along the boardwalk, flourishing in the sunnier places. Eventually you'll find yourself in an alder swamp. Well-known to hunters, trappers, and others who venture off trail in the north, these large shrubs(and sometimes trees) grow in a tangled, dense mass that is all but impenetrable. The biggest alder (*Alnus rugosa*)

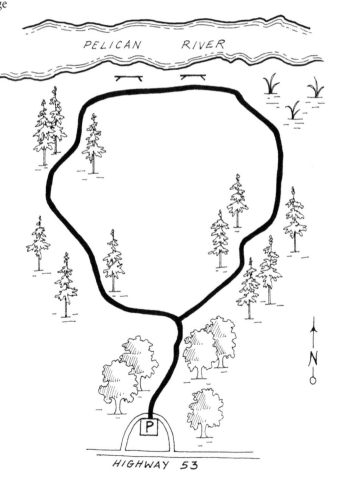

Legend

Parking	P
Trail	—
Bench	⌒
Marsh	⅄

in the nation grows in Michigan and measures just over 1 foot in diameter and 66 feet high. See, they can become trees.

As you continue your walk, the alder will be replaced by willow and cattail as the predominate plants, the trees finally giving way to lower-growing vegetation. Another plant that has taken hold here, although pretty in bloom, doesn't belong and is unwelcome. Purple loosestrife has invaded this area, as it has bogs and marshes all over the eastern United States. It supplants native vegetation, particularly cattail. Since lots of different wildlife use cattail and associated plants for food and shelter, biologists are worried about loosestrife's impact.

Here the walkway enters an open area were you can see the Pelican River. Two obvious plants near the edge of the open water are pickerel weed and American lotus flower, the latter more commonly known as lily pads. Lots of birds also frequent the river. Bald eagles feed here, as do canvasback and mallard ducks, great blue herons, grebes, and even white pelicans.

There are a couple of benches along this section of the walk. If you have time, sit down and wait. Sitting still and silently is always the best way of seeing wildlife. As the walkway curves its way back onto dryer ground, you'll notice a little thicket of bog birch, a diminutive birch tree with spatula-shaped leaves that loves this moist ground.

Leaving the wet river area behind, you'll enter a peat bog, covered at ground level with sphagnum moss. This moss is what becomes peat, and in some areas of the state it has accumulated to a depth of over 100 feet. Above you are black spruce, trees that you've seen before on this walk, but here they grow in an almost pure stand. They also grow very slowly; some of the bigger ones are over 100 years old.

Because this ground is very acidic, some of the vegetation growing here is unique. Labrador tea is a plant whose leaves and buds look quite like those of a rhododendron. It's a widely distributed plant in the north, and you'll see lots of it in northern Minnesota. Harder to see here is bog rosemary, which is shorter, rarely getting over 1 foot tall. It has long, almost needlelike leaves. The best time to spot it is in June, when its pinkish-white blossoms grab your attention. Almost impossible to find but worth looking for is the small cranberry (*Vaccinium oxycoccus*). This very low-growing, vining evergreen plant produces small, pea-sized red fruit related to our beloved Thanksgiving cranberry.

As you continue, you'll experience yet another change in scenery, first walking among black spruce mixed with tamarack, then once again into the black ash swamp. It is here that the boardwalk reconnects at the junction you passed earlier. Bear right and you'll reach the parking area where you began the walk.

Bog Walk
Lake Bemidji State Park

Distance: 3 miles, round trip

Time: 1.5 hours

Path: This is an easy walk, with nearly a mile of it on a boardwalk. Most of the rest is over level ground on a sandy, mowed surface. There are several junctions but they are well marked.

Directions: From the junction of Highway 197 and County Highway 21 in Bemidji, take 21 north approximately 5 miles to County Highway 20. Go right (east) 1.7 miles on 20 to the park entrance on the right.

Contact: Lake Bemidji State Park, 3401 State Park Road N.E., Bemidji, MN 56601; (218)755-3843.

Highlights: A nearly half-mile-long boardwalk takes you on a tour of a tranquil bog and leads you to a lovely little lake. This is a peaceful walk into a place that's unique and full of discovery.

Start walking from the campground parking area at the far end of the camp road. There's a large signboard at the trailhead, which will point you in the correct direction. The trail is actually an old road, still used for snowmobiling in winter. It is wide and not particularly inviting, but bear with its lack of aesthetic appeal for a bit the bog walk is worth it.

You'll cross Highway 20 and then take the right-most trail. It's signed and easy to find but a bit less wide. The woods are a mixture of dry sand-loving plants, including jack pine, northern pin oak, some bigger red pine, and lots of hazel brush for an understory. Just a few hundred feet down the trail you can see an old red pine skeleton on the left, to which a worn footpath leads. The curved trunk of this old pine, dead for some time, is ideal for sitting on, a fact that probably hastened its demise.

You'll soon come to the first of many illustrated signboards along the trail. This one tells about the white pine, one of which sits about 10 feet in front of and just to the left of the sign. Then the trail breaks into an opening in the forest, one that's been replanted with red pine that are about 10 feet tall. Note that the path here is very sandy. These are glacial soils deposited by the last ice sheet 10,000 years ago.

At the next signboard, which informs you about quaking aspen, listen as you read. If there is even a slight breeze, you'll hear the aspen above you whisper in a timeless language, one that may say more to you than the sign.

Next you'll come to the junction for the bog trail. The trail sign here makes it hard to miss the turn. Bear right and you'll find that the trail, now still narrower than before, takes you up and down a couple of swales. Then you'll come to another large signboard, similar to the one at the beginning of the trail. It points you down a well-worn dirt path that dips into a lowland in about 100 feet.

Suddenly you'll find yourself in a bog. Walk out onto the boardwalk and begin your excursion into a unique and wonderful plant community, on a trail that's really been done right. Immediately you'll notice that some of the leafy plants act as if they want to join you up on the boardwalk. Dogwood, alder, and bog birch flourish here and crowd the walkway with their branches. Overhead, tamarack and black spruce provide the only tall cover.

Just a few feet farther on the boardwalk, you'll encounter two large signboards bearing color pictures of lovely bog plants like marsh marigold, bog cranberry, and Minnesota's state flower, showy lady's slipper. Such "field guide" quality illustrations are expensive and difficult to maintain. Let the park authorities know you appreciate their efforts in providing them.

The next signboard is especially fascinating. It's titled "Bog Canopy" and discusses tamarack and black spruce. It also displays a core sample taken from a puny, 8-inch-diameter black spruce near the sign. The rings on the sample show that the tree is 97 years old!

Continue your stroll out into this wet place, and you'll learn from yet another signboard that the word *bog* comes from the Celtic word *bocc*, meaning "soft." If you've ever stepped in a bog, you'll appreciate the derivation. As you're walking along, you may notice an 8-foot section of boardwalk planks that are different from the all others. They are a different color, brown, and they are a bit slippery. These, according to the sign, were made from recycled plastic: 1,200 recycled milk jugs to be exact.

As the walkway approaches Big Bog Lake, the bog, not surprisingly, gets wetter. Channels of water appear near the path, and there are more cattails. Soon the lake is visible through the trees off to the left. Walk out to the turnaround loop and sit on the bench for a while. And sit in silence. The longer and more patiently you wait, the more likely it is that you'll see wildlife of some sort: tiny warblers, great blue herons, frogs, turtles, coyotes, and perhaps even a moose. Enjoy the respite before your leisurely stroll back to the parking area.

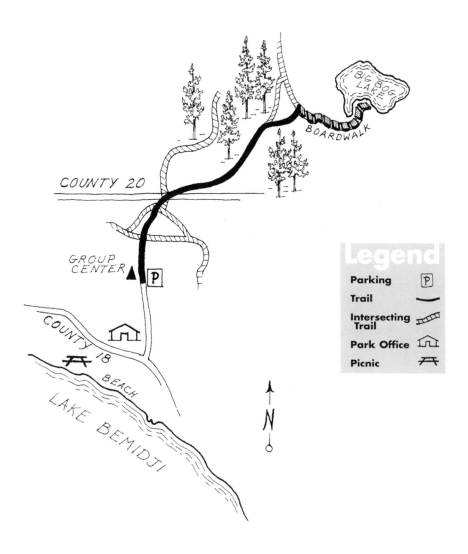

BIG BOG LAKE

BOARDWALK

COUNTY 20

GROUP CENTER ▲ P

COUNTY 18

BEACH

LAKE BEMIDJI

N

Legend

Parking P
Trail
Intersecting Trail
Park Office
Picnic

Bog Walk
Hayes Lake State Park

Distance: Slightly less than 1 mile

Time: 30 minutes

Path: The walk through the bog is on a boardwalk, and the path to it is down a wide path of mowed grass. The junctions are well marked, but getting to the trailhead is tricky. See the description of the beginning of the hike for guidance.

Directions: From the intersection of Highways 89, 11, and 310 in Roseau, take 89 south approximately 14.5 miles to County Highway 4. Go east on County 4 for 8 miles to the park entrance on the right.

Contact: Hayes Lake State Park , 48990 County Road 4, Roseau, MN 56751; (218)425-7504.

Highlights: This short stroll, the shortest in this book, is included because it takes you into a bog whose canopy is comprised of northern white cedar, which is common in the North Woods but usually difficult to find because of its penchant for growing in wet and inaccessible places. But, ironically, almost everyone knows this plant because it grows in many city environments, often next to front doors.

Start your hike from the campground next to Campsite 17, at the Pine Ridge Trail, although there is no sign at the entrance. The woods here are full of jack pine, aspen, balsam fir, and white spruce, and Hayes Lake is visible through the trees on the right. You'll also notice a remarkable white spruce just off the trail toward the lake, located at the margin of the white cedar bog you're about to hike into. It's gigantic, maybe 100 feet tall and about 8 feet around.

You'll soon pass a junction with the Bear Track Trail, which cuts off to the left. Go right at the junction, down a hill, and you'll see a sign that directs you to the boardwalk; a larger signboard there tells you about the walk.

The boardwalk is similar to a pier jutting out into a lake. Sections of wood planking have been placed on uprights that have been driven into the ground. The boardwalk makes for an easy walking surface and protects the delicate plants below from hundreds, even thousands of footfalls. As the signboard says, a footprint here can last for years in the spongy moss, which is mostly sphagnum, common in northern bogs. Over millennia, it forms extensive peat beds, which can become hundreds of feet thick.

Some small plants that grow in the moss and in the peat below it are the Labrador tea, whose leaves and buds resemble those of a rhododendron, bog rosemary, and pitcher plant, a carnivorous plant that attracts, traps, and digests flies and other insects.

As you walk down the boardwalk, you'll see a signboard that explains that some of the planks below are made from the plastic of recycled milk jugs. Think about that the next time you slug down some two percent!

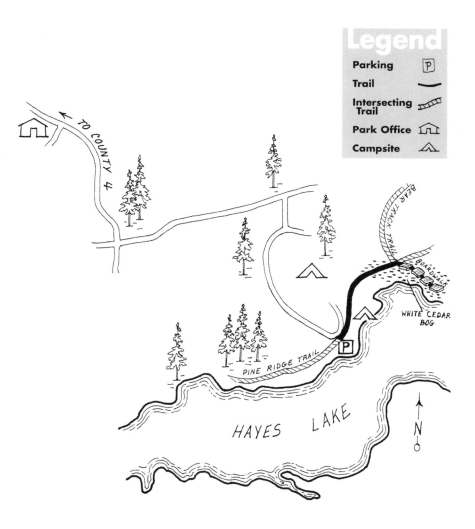

The next signboard is a long, rectangular affair with color pictures of some of the plants and animals you may encounter. Unless you walk here in the spring, you'll miss the orchids, but the pictures help give you a feel for what happens during the entire growing season.

Behind this signboard about 10 feet is a white cedar with a 15-inch diameter that is the biggest tree of its kind on this walk and is perhaps over 100 years old. Most things in a bog grow slowly because there is lots of competition for the limited sunlight, and the soil, mostly peat, is very infertile. In addition, this particular bog can experience freezing temperatures in every month of the year; and so you have a very hostile place for living things.

The end of the boardwalk is not far from the big cedar. You can peer into the dark, deep recess of the bog and imagine deer sneaking though it or perhaps a black bear prowling it in search of a den. Take a deep breath and smell the unique fragrance, a blend of musty peat moss and almost sweet cedar boughs. It's a fragrance you'll never forget.

When you're ready, walk back on the boardwalk and find the dirt trail you came here on. Turn left and you'll be heading back to where you parked.

Riverside
Rambles

Silver Creek Trail
Jay Cooke State Park

Distance: 3.5 miles

Time: 1.5 to 2 hours

Path: As wide as a country road, it has a dirt or grass surface and can be muddy, even slippery, in the spring or after summer rains. The trail is well marked, with signboards at the junctions.

Directions: From the intersection of I-35 and Highway 210 just south of Cloquet, take Highway 210 approximately 6 miles east. After the road enters the park, go approximately 3 miles to the park headquarters and picnic area on the right.

Contact: Jay Cooke State Park, 500 East Highway 210, Carlton, MN 55718; (218) 384-4610.

Highlights: The St. Louis River and two billion years of history are the attractions here. There's also a "swinging" bridge and a hillside full of yellow lady slippers.

Start your hike from the parking lot adjacent to the headquarters and picnic area. The bridge over the St. Louis River is due south, visible from the lot. As you cross the swinging bridge you'll note that it does swing . . . and bounce and creak. Even if you don't have a weak stomach, you probably don't want to stand in the middle of the span for very long; motion sickness will strike quickly. The bridge was washed out in the spring of 1950 from floodwaters. The *Duluth News-Tribune* noted that the only thing left after the flood was "a mass of twisted steel and splintered footboards." When rebuilt three years later, the structure was raised a couple of feet with the installation of concrete caps, which are visible on the bridge's suspension piers.

In the water below, you'll see massive rock slabs, tilted 40 to 70 degrees from the horizontal. These are made of slate, a type of Precambrian rock formed from marine sediments deposited beneath a gigantic sea two billion years ago. With time and enormous pressure, the mud metamorphosed into shale, then into the harder slate. With more time and pressure, the slate was tilted to the various angles you see below.

During wet periods, when there's lots of water coursing down the St. Louis, fewer of these rocks are visible. It is this torrent of water that has exposed these old rocks, sweeping away countless tons of more recent glacial silt and sand deposits. Look down the river valley and note how wide it is. That width is the result not of today's river but of a glacial river that drained a glacier's meltwater 10,000 years ago.

More recently, the Ojibwa called the river Kitchigumizibi, which means "Lake Superior River." Its headwaters are 160 miles northwest, in Seven Beaver Lake, southeast of Babbit, Minnesota. The St. Louis was part of the famous trail that the voyageurs used to reach the Mississippi, but this part of the river was too dangerous for them to navigate. (See the section "In the Footsteps of the Voyageurs" in this book for more on these early pioneers.) The river drops 498 feet on its cascade through the park, almost half of its total elevation loss of 1,067 feet. The 9-mile portage used by the voyageurs traces an east-

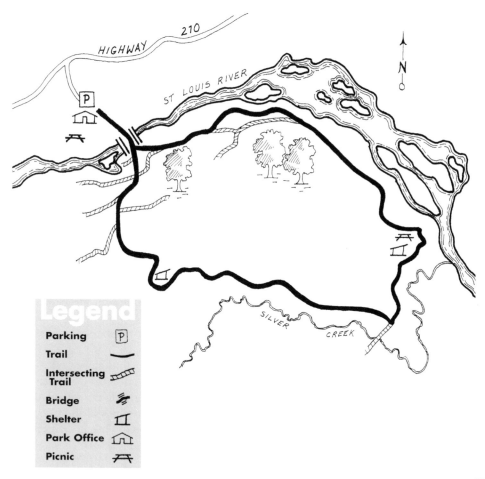

Legend

Parking	P
Trail	—
Intersecting Trail	
Bridge	
Shelter	
Park Office	
Picnic	

west path and lies mostly north of the park, with a small segment within its northeast boundary.

When you've had enough of ancient rocks and glacial torrents, finish crossing the bridge and you'll be on the south bank. Take the left-most trail, which is the Silver Creek Trail. After climbing a few steps made from wooden railroad tie, you'll enter the wide trail. You'll be walking parallel to the river but at a height of 75 to 100 feet above it for the next half mile or so. Trees will block your view in most places, but there are a couple of places where you can walk to the edge of the cliff. These afford a glimpse of the quarter-mile-wide river valley, strewn with boulders during low flow and rife with whitewater during high.

When you reach a shelter and picnic table, take a break and enjoy the view. Silver Creek twists 45 feet below on the way to its confluence with the St. Louis. Depending on the season, you may see trout fishermen plying this clear little stream for their wily quarry. As you leave the shelter area, you'll begin a gradual climb up and away from the St. Louis, with the trail roughly paralleling Silver Creek but well above it. When you reach the next trail junction and signboard, bear right and stay on the Silver Creek Trail.

Continue your gradual climb and you'll reach a wide wooden bridge that spans a little stream trickling from a beaver pond on your right. The beaver's dam is massive, spanning at least 50 yards and rising three or four feet above the ground. The beaver's lodge, a hodgepodge of sticks and limbs, sits in the middle of the pond.

Your climb steepens a bit as the trail curves around and up a hillside. There's a shelter and picnic table about halfway up the hill. In mid-May, the hillside is home to blooming yellow lady's slipper, a native orchid.

Beyond the top of the hill you'll arrive at another trail junction. Bear right and the trail will take you into an area where there are some bigger trees. Many of them, yellow birch, but also the red oak, have damaged tops, perhaps from a storm 20 or 30 years ago. Go straight at the next trail junction. After about 100 feet, look for a white cedar immediately next to the trail that has several large elongated holes gouged into its trunk, with one being about six feet off the ground. These were made by North America's largest woodpecker, the pileated.

You'll soon hear river sounds, which means you are almost back to the swinging bridge. But take one last detour. Look for a path that leads left, out to the river. If the water isn't too high, you can scramble over the giant tilted slate slabs and get a close-up view of the river. When you reach the bridge, set it creaking again as you hike back over it and then to your car, or to a waiting picnic if you planned ahead.

Two Rivers Trail
St. Croix State Park

Distance: 3.8 miles

Time: 2 hours

Path: Varies from a wide mowed-grass road to an almost nonexistent footpath. This is a difficult hike into a remote area. Poison ivy is common along the trail and even on the trail. Dress and plan accordingly.

Directions: From Hinckley take Highway 48 east 15 miles to County Highway 22. Go right on Highway 22 for 5 miles to the park entrance.

Contact: St. Croix State Park, Route 3, Box 450, Hinckley, MN 55037; (320)384-6591.

Highlights: Much of what Minnesota's largest state park (33,000 acres)has to offer: the confluence of the Kettle and the St. Croix Rivers that is usually visited only by canoeists; a lovely and remote setting; abundant and diverse vegetation and wildlife all in an area that's accessible from urban centers.

St. Croix State Park is bounded on the south and east by 21 miles of the St. Croix River and on the west by the Kettle River, which was Minnesota's first waterway to receive Federal Wild and Scenic River designation. The park's most popular hike is on an easy 2.3-mile trail along the St. Croix on which hikers are never more than .2 mile from the park road. Rather than do that, we'll take you on a trek to the confluence of the St. Croix and Kettle Rivers.

You'll reach the head of Two Rivers Trail by driving the park road almost to its end, about 11 miles. When you see the Kettle River Overlook sign, it's .9 mile to the start of the Two Rivers Trail. Park on the right and don't block the gate.

The first half mile of trail is a grass-covered road used for access to the Pine Ridge canoe campsite. You hike through mostly deciduous trees, a few big oak, and occasional pine. The understory you'll walk through consists of hazel, ironwood, blue beach, willow, and other brushy small trees and shrubs. About a quarter of a mile into the hike you'll trek through an enormous stand of wild sarsparilla, a foot-tall native wildflower with three leafstalks, each of which contains five leaves.

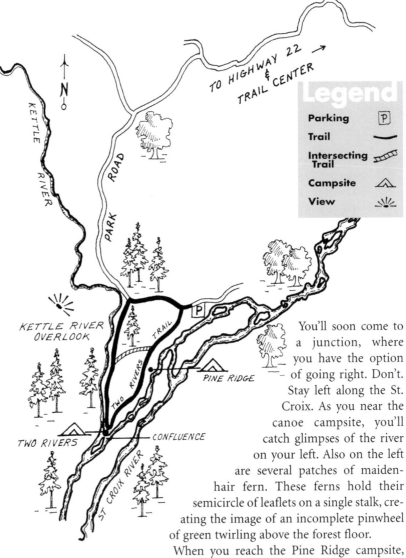

You'll soon come to a junction, where you have the option of going right. Don't. Stay left along the St. Croix. As you near the canoe campsite, you'll catch glimpses of the river on your left. Also on the left are several patches of maidenhair fern. These ferns hold their semicircle of leaflets on a single stalk, creating the image of an incomplete pinwheel of green twirling above the forest floor.

When you reach the Pine Ridge campsite, you'll understand how it got its name. A giant white pine stands near the landing, and several others form a 100-foot-high wall on the opposite riverbank. There's a fire ring and picnic table at this site, so if you brought food, you can eat it in comfort. The trail heading out from the site is much different from the one that brought you here. The new stretch is a narrow footpath, unmowed and little used. You can find it if you walk near the river.

If you look downriver you can see an island, with 60-foot-long tree trunks jammed against the upstream side. Spring floods here vastly increase the river's flow and scour the banks and floodplain.

The trail runs along a slightly elevated mound of dirt that serves as a riverbank between the flowing river and the more tranquil bottomland. It is very meadowlike, with scattered trees, but mostly grasses, flowers, willow, and hazel brush (and poison ivy!). If you examine some of the trees near the river, you'll see that their bark has been damaged from ground level up to about three or four feet. This was caused by floating debris crashing into them and abrading the bark during spring high water.

As you hike, be careful whenever you come to wood planks that have been placed over small gullies. Some of these planks have twisted lengthwise and, because they're obscured by vegetation, may surprise and cause a twisted ankle or unwanted fall. Injury in this remote spot could be more than a mere inconvenience.

Another notable site along your way will be beaver trails. As these large (up to 60 pound) rodents carry out their engineering plans, they drag lots of tree parts from inland to the river. In doing so they make well-worn runways, far more worn than the trail you're hiking on.

When you begin seeing openings in the forest on the right, you're nearing the Kettle River, and in only 100 yards or so, the peninsula that marks the mingling of it with the St. Croix. Stand on the bank and look across the two rivers. Lovely white pine line their banks, a fitting circumstance given that, before logging, this area supported thousands of such trees. In fact, this spot may appear very similar today to what it looked like to Dakota or Ojibwa hunters as they made their way south to winter hunting areas. Immerse yourself, literally if you'd like, in the merging of two great and historic rivers.

When you're ready, head up the Kettle. The path is a bit more noticeable than the one down the St. Croix. And because the bank is higher and dryer, there is less brush and grass to contend with. You'll walk through an expansive grove of pine, mostly red, that has a parklike feel to it. Pine needles make a soft, quiet carpet under the tall, reddish, limbless-to-40-feet tree trunks. On a hot day pine scent pervades the air.

Farther up the river, you'll have to navigate around a beaver dam that sits almost squarely on the trail, flooding about a quarter of an acre. Either walk over the dam or around on the river side of it, and you can easily find the trail again.

When you reach a junction with a cutoff that leads to the St. Croix, head left, staying close to the Kettle. You'll pass through another pine grove, less parklike than the first, and then see a tangle of beaver-felled aspen. You'll occasionally hear the sound of the Kettle getting louder, a result of the greater abundance of rocks in this section of river. You'll soon reach the park road very near the Kettle River Overlook. If you turn right onto the road, it's a little less than a mile to your vehicle.

River Trail
Wild River State Park

Distance: 3 miles

Time: 1 to 2 hours

Path: An easy stroll, mostly on mowed grass, with good trail markings.

Directions: From Taylors Falls, take Highway 95 about 10 miles northwest to the intersection with County Highway 12 in Almelund. Turn right (north) on Highway 12 and go about 3 miles to the park entrance.

Contact: Wild River State Park, 39797 Park Trail, Center City, MN 55012; (651)583-2125.

Highlights: The old Nevers Dam site is fascinating and full of historic significance. When in bloom, the wildflower meadow near the middle of this hike is also wonderful.

To reach your first goal of getting to Amik's Pond Trail, begin your hike at the end of the parking area near the visitor center. The path is wide and sandy at first, then it turns grassy. You'll soon pass a junction with Windfall Trail on the left. At the second junction, marked by a sign announcing Amik's Pond Trail, bear right and begin descending through an oak woods. The hillside under the forest canopy is covered with ferns. Near the end of your descent, you'll encounter another junction, this one where Amik's Pond Trail loops back left and connects with itself. Bear right and walk down a very straight section of trail.

The trail is so straight because it was originally constructed as a road in 1849 to connect the city of St. Paul with Lake Superior. Before the road was built, the only commercial and military route between the city and the lake required travelers to paddle upstream on the St. Croix River, make a difficult portage, and then paddle down the Bois Brule River to Lake Superior. There's one tree along the path that may have witnessed some of the road traffic in those early days. Watch for a two-stemmed white oak, with both stems measuring more than 3 feet in diameter, located at the right side of the next trail junction, across from the map board.

Turn left at this junction. You'll then emerge into a meadow. Blackberries tangle on the right, bearing more fruit per plant than you'll probably ever see. Some of the flowers that grow here include bergamot, milkweed, mullein, black-eyed Susan, daisy fleabane, great Saint-John's-wort, and Culver's root. The show is impressive.

As you proceed through the prairie, you'll suddenly realize that the river is just in front of you. This is an impressive and uncommonly open approach to a river that is usually cloaked in trees. At the bench set along the trail here, sit and enjoy the river for a while. That's Wisconsin across the water, Governor Knowles State Forest to be exact. Back on the trail, you'll cross a small, usually dry creek bed, the outlet from Amik's Pond. With the St. Croix on your right and a large meadow to the left, hike until you reach the boat launch and canoe concession. Here Amik's Pond Trail goes left and the River Trail begins. You want to continue upriver so proceed straight. There's an old dam and spillway with a bridge over them. Look down into the water and see if you can spot any fish. Deer also frequent this spot toward evening, so if you're quiet you might surprise one or it might surprise you!

As the trail follows the small creek for a while, note the wild grapevines cascading over small trees and shrubs, making trellises out of hapless plants.

ST. CROIX RIVER

OLD NEVERS DAM SITE

OLD LOGGING TRAIL

RIVER TRAIL

COUNTY 12

AMIK'S POND

Legend

Parking   P

Trail

Intersecting Trail

Campsite

55

When the path dips down into a little wet swale, note the cattails to the left. A couple of Turks cap lilies grow near the trail here. If you're lucky enough to find them and they are blooming, examine their orange down-turned blossom and their unusual "Turk's cap."

When you reach the canoe campsite along the riverbank, you're about to enter a long, relatively straight section of trail that runs through a river bottomland. Various types of water-tolerant trees flourish here: basswood, hackberry black ash, and silver maple all tolerate wet feet, roots covered for days in the spring by high river water. Many trees would die under such condition, but these trees like it. So do several types of vines, the most prominent of which is Virginia creeper, with its five-swirled leaflets. Others include poison ivy (growing thick near the trail in some places) and Dutchman's pipe. Grape also run rampant in places that aren't quite as wet.

When you reach the next trail junction, turn right out to the river and the site of the old Nevers Dam. Signboards describe the dam, which was built in 1889 to help hold back and control the flood of logs farther downriver. The world's largest logjam occurred a few miles downstream at Taylors Falls in 1886. (See the Interstate State Park hike later in this book for more on this event.) Nevers Dam had been the world's largest pile-driven dam. Giant steam driven pile drivers smashed telephone-pole-size tree trunks into the river bottom to form the foundation of the dam. Used for only a decade or so as a logging dam, the structure deteriorated and was removed in 1954.

Hike back to the junction and head away from the river. The structure you're walking on was an integral part of the Nevers Dam. This 660-foot-long dike, constructed of soil and rock excavated from the bluffs up ahead, was built to prevent spring floodwaters from circumventing the dam through the river's floodplain.

After you climb back up to higher ground out of the floodplain, you'll reach a picnic grounds. Bear left until you reach the Old Logging Trail and reenter the woods. This path parallels the River Trail but runs above the floodplain. It is also long and straight and will take you quickly back to the visitor center. Make sure you check out the native wildflower garden when you get there. Many prairie plants are on display and identified so you can better recognize them out in the field.

Riverside Walk
William O'Brien State Park

Distance: 1.5 miles

Time: 1 hour

Path: Mostly mowed grass and wood chips. The trail is well marked and quite easy.

Directions: From Stillwater on the St. Croix River, take Highway 95 about 15 miles north to the park entrance.

Contact: William O'Brien State Park, 16821 O'Brien Trail North, Marine on St. Croix, MN 55047; (651)433-0500.

Highlights: This is a tranquil trek with great views of the always-stunning St. Croix River, especially of some massive pines that seem to defy gravity as they lean over the surging water.

Start walking from the park beach, across the road from the parking lot, on the east shore of Lake Alice. Walk north past the picnic pavilion and through a natural arch made of sumac. Note how clear the water is, even though it's very weedy. The lake is named after the daughter of William O'Brien, who donated 180 acres for park development in 1945.

You'll hike briefly along the park road, between it and the lake. Before you cross the road, note the dense growth of horsetail covering the ground like porcupine quills. Just after crossing the road, you'll notice some large red oak trees near the trail. Running beside the trail for a bit is small brook that bubbles and splashes as it travels its last few yards before mingling with the spectacular St. Croix River.

When you get to the river's edge, hike left for about 10 yards for a good view upriver. Imagine what the area must have looked like in 1830 before the lumbermen came. It would have been sheltered by massive pine rising 100 feet and more into the air. Now you'll see just a few such giants. Walk back to the trail and continue south down along the river. Take one of the paths that lead to the water and look across to the Wisconsin side.

As you move south, you'll see a small island perched in the middle of the river, then the north end of a larger island. This larger one is Greenberg Island, donated by David Greenberg in 1958. Accessible only by boat, it serves as a haven for wild things. When the river is high in the spring, however, the entire island can be submerged. When that happens, most wildlife, such as deer, swim to shore until the water subsides. Other, less land-bound creatures like birds and squirrels take to the trees.

Soon you'll reach an area near the campground where big white pine still hold sway. And sway they do. If it's windy you can see the branches and even the upper trunk move back and forth. There are a few trees here that lean precipitously out over the river. As spring floods erode the soil from beneath them, they tip gradually riverward. Given their already serious tilt, it's amazing more of them don't just flop into the water.

When you reach the picnic tables, look for a big hackberry tree on the right, then a butternut hickory on the left. Walk past the park's outdoor amphitheater and another pavilion by the boat launch, then along the shore of Lake Alice. If it's a warm day you'll hear the sound of kids frolicking on the beach. That means you've completed your walk at William O'Brien.

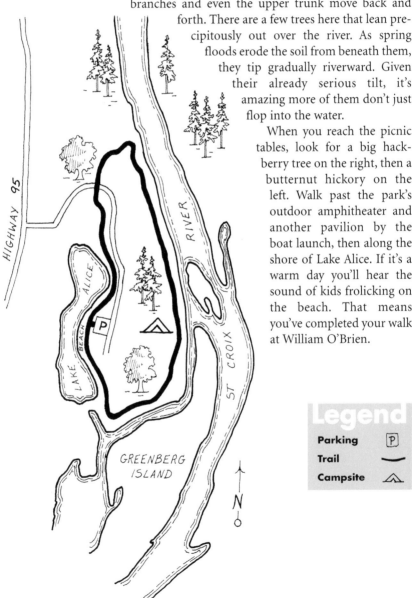

HIGHWAY 95

RIVER

ST CROIX

LAKE ALICE BEACH

P

GREENBERG ISLAND

N

Legend

Parking	P
Trail	—
Campsite	⌂

North Railroad Grade and Backpacking Loops
Afton State Park

Distance: 4 miles

Time: 2 hours

Path: There is a variety of surfaces on this hike, from mowed grass, to asphalt, to railroad grade gravel, to mowed prairie. The trails are well marked, but pay attention at the numerous intersections or you may be off on your own hike (which may not be so bad).

Directions: From the intersection of I-94 and County Highway 15 about 8 miles east of St. Paul, go south on Highway 15 for 7 miles to County Highway 20. Take Highway 20 east (left) 3 miles to the park entrance.

Contact: Afton State Park, 6959 Peller Avenue South, Hastings, MN 55033; (651)436-5391.

Highlights: This is a surprisingly wild and natural place given its proximity to a large metropolitan area. Close-ups of lovely blooming wildflowers combined with distant vistas of rolling bluffs and the St. Croix River Valley make this a visually stunning hike.

This hike starts from the parking area at the end of the park road. Walk through the picnic area into the woods. Stay left past the picnic shelter, then take a right at a Y intersection. As you walk down the asphalt path, you can see a low area off to the left and, through the trees, the Afton Alps ski area in the distance. The first overlook on the right gives you a glimpse of the broad St. Croix River, which at this point is only about 6 miles from its confluence with the Mississippi.

After the overlook, you'll descend a series of steps. At the bottom, the path becomes gravel. The trail, actually an old railroad grade, is very straight for the next half mile or so. Note how the terrain drops off on both sides. Fill was hauled in so that the river wouldn't flood the tracks in times of high water. You'll see enormous multistemmed silver maple on the left and similar sized eastern cottonwood on the right. Both sides of the trail may be underwater if the river is high.

When you reach a picnic grounds on the right, walk through it and toward the river. You'll soon see a beach; take a short stroll along it or take a dip if you'd like. When you're ready, find one of the worn paths that leads back up to the trail grade and continue hiking by turning right onto the path. You'll cross a bridge, which you will hike under on your way back. Then resume your trek down the rest of the half-mile railroad grade, with the river on the right and a steep hillside on the left.

When you reach the next bridge, you'll know it's nearly time to turn left and head up onto the bluffs. The railroad grade will continue, but follow the arrow that points uphill away from the river. The climbing path here is narrower. There are two pitches to this 150-foot-climb, with a 100-yard-long respite in the middle. Once at the top, you'll emerge into an open field, where the trail hugs the edge of the trees, then cuts across the field toward a trail junction. If you take a left detour at this junction for a couple of hundred yards, through rows of pines, you'll reach an overlook. The view is to the south, downriver, near the park headquarters. The high-voltage power lines you can see pass over the trail near the trailhead. After this brief side trip, retrace your route back to the field.

After continuing down the mowed path, you'll reach a bench. Turn around and look back, and you'll be able to gaze upon at least two bluff lines in the distance and a farm on the Wisconsin side of the river. As you tread the gently looping path, you'll see a variety of wildflowers, depending on the time of year. In July, the area here will be alive with penstemon, blue vervain, milkweed, lesser Saint-John's-wort, bergamot, and common mullein in full bloom. Up ahead, you'll also notice the path leading to a pair of stone pillars that used to support a gate. This is the site of an old homestead, and just past the pillars on the left are some farm implements and the remains of an old windmill.

When you reach the next junction, bear left and follow the sign with only the image of a hiker on it. You'll pass briefly through some woods, then be back into the open again, before you make a steep, quadriceps-bursting descent into yet another field. You'll quickly reach the edge of a bluff, the last one before you return to the river. On the edge of the clearing, near where the trail turns right and parallels the bluff top, you'll find leadplant, one of the few nonherbaceous prairie plants. Its fine-textured, silvery green leaflets contrast with the iridescent purple flowers peeking from the end of its branchlets.

The trail briefly traces the bluff top, then makes a final drop down to the river. Once near the bottom, you'll pass under the same bridge you did on the first part of the trek. Then simply go right and climb back up onto the railroad grade that you walked earlier. Retrace you steps and head home.

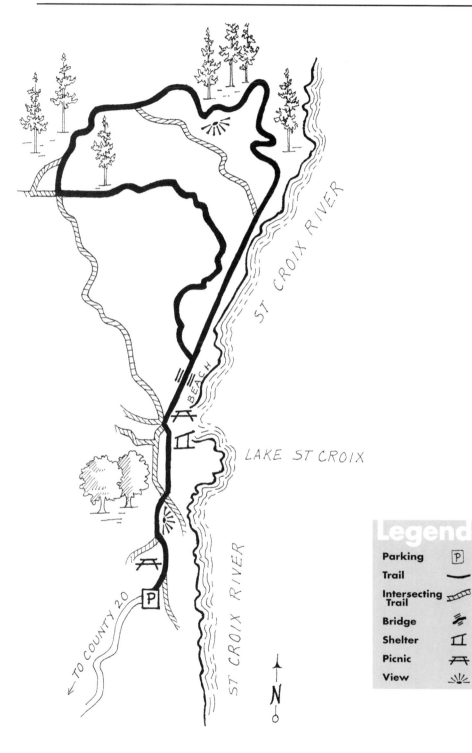

ST CROIX RIVER

BEACH

LAKE ST CROIX

ST CROIX RIVER

TO COUNTY 20

N

Legend

Parking [P]
Trail
Intersecting Trail
Bridge
Shelter
Picnic
View

Third Bridge to the Second Bridge, via North Meadow Trail
Oxbow Park

Distance: 3 miles

Time: 1 to 2 hours

Path: Mostly woodland and worn dirt, with some grass. The trail crosses two bridges and climbs and descends a bluff. It's easy to follow.

Directions: From the intersection of Highway 14 and County Highway 5 in Byron, take Highway 5 north for 3 miles to the intersection with County Highway 4. Go straight on County Road 105 and take it north into the park.

Contact: Oxbow Park, 5731 County Road 105, Byron, MN 55920; (507)775-2451.

Highlights: From river bottom to bluff top, this walk provides glimpses of diverse natural niches along and above the impressive Zumbro River. The Oxbow Nature Center and the Zollman Zoo are well maintained and inviting, well worth a visit.

Start your walk from the Nature Center parking lot. Head toward a row of red pine located at the northeast corner of the Nature Center, where you'll come to a path between the pines and a row of large amur maples on the right. You'll then exit the pines into a picnic and play area. Head toward the bridge you'll see ahead. This is where you'll cross the Zumbro River and enter the Zumbro Trail.

The "3rd Bridge," as it's called, affords you an opportunity to view the lovely river. The Zumbro consists of several forks and branches, one of which runs through Rochester, 12 miles east of here. The stream that courses through the park is the South Branch of the Middle Fork of the Zumbro River. It's a pleasant body of water that, when eventually connected with all its brethren branches and forks, forms an impressive river that winds toward the great Mississippi, eventually merging with it just south of Wabasha.

Across the bridge several large black walnut trees lord over a verdant river-bottom understory. The trail climbs gradually to about 50 feet above the river, where it meets with the North Meadow Trail. A

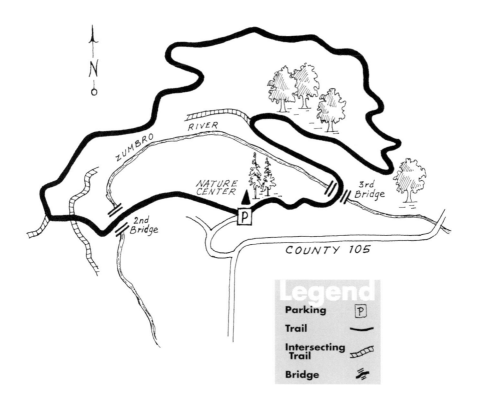

Legend

Parking	P
Trail	—
Intersecting Trail	
Bridge	

sign identifies the trails and declares the distance . . . in feet! So don't panic when you read that the North Meadow Trail you are about to traverse is 10,265 feet long. That's really only 1.9 miles. The North Meadow Trail heads back up the hillside above the Zumbro Trail we have been on. Approximately 20 yards past the trail junction and 10 yards deep into the woods on the left is a basswood tree growing out of a chunk of rock. One wonders how it got there and how it survives.

Keep moving up the trail into an open area full of small trees, mostly aspen. You'll encounter several switchbacks as the trail climbs to the top of the bluff and crosses through patches of raspberry, sumac, and small black walnut trees. You'll see an old fence that marks the park boundary, and then a bench from which there's a nice view up the coulee. This marks the top of the bluff, after which you'll hike through a stand of large black walnut, then into some enormous white oak.

The trail crosses and skirts an old farm field that park personnel are converting to prairie. You may see fire lanes mowed around the edge. Fire is one of the critical features of prairie, serving to kill invading trees and shrubs and favoring prairie grasses and forbs. You'll pass a thicket of hawthorn trees and another of prickly ash, a particularly nasty plant whose stout one-inch thorns make a stand of them virtually impenetrable. The trail circles a coulee, then heads back across the old field into and down four rows of pine, three white and one red, until it returns to the bluff edge. The river is below, and the trail dips into several ravines. Look up the ravines and you'll see a farm field from which water runs off, creating the erosive gullies you're crossing.

The trail makes a gradual decent off the bluff to a junction. The Maple Trail continues south along the bluff. You'll turn left and head past a junction with the Zumbro Trail on your way to the "2nd," or middle, bridge. Just past the Zumbro Trail junction there are some wood steps, crafted to curve down the hillside in a lovely arc. Look back up at them when you reach the bottom to get the full effect.

Once on the floodplain, you'll wind your way between hackberry and silver maple trees to the bridge, which has steps leading up to it. As you can probably guess, the bridge was constructed high over the water to avoid being washed away by spring floods. After you cross it, you'll be in a grassy picnic area. By staying left between the river and the road, you'll arrive at the campground between sites 16 and 17. Walk across the circle in the middle of the campground road. The trail continues from behind site 5. After passing through a couple of rows of pine and into a field, you'll find the Nature Center parking lot where you started.

Prairie
Paths

Around the River Hike
Buffalo River State Park

Distance: 3 miles

Time: 1.5 to 2 hours

Path: Easy to follow, along mowed grass and prairie, with a few sections worn down to dirt. A few hundred yards are on an old asphalt road. Most of the trail is flat, except for a few hills you'll encounter entering and leaving the riverbed. The section of trail along the river can be very wet during high water in spring.

Directions: From Moorhead go west on Highway 10 for about 12 miles to the park entrance on the right. A state park sticker is required.

Contact: Buffalo River State Park, P.O. Box 352, Glyndon, MN 56547; (218)498-2124.

Highlights: This is a delightful stroll through a river bottom forest and a vast stand of big bluestem grass. As you can imagine, the Buffalo River area was once populated by bison. Today, their bones are still occasionally found in the sediment along the river.

Start this hike from the picnic grounds adjacent to the large parking area near the middle of the park. Head south, past the swimming area on your left. In less than a quarter mile, you'll come to a bridge across the Buffalo River; cross it and bear left up the opposite side. As you cross, don't forget to scan the eroding banks for bison skulls.

The woods around you are typical of river bottom forest in this area of the state. Elm, oak, ash, basswood, and cottonwood are the major shade-givers here. As you leave the river bottom, climbing vertically about 15 feet, you'll hike through a transition zone where aspen and wild plum give way to open, treeless prairie.

You'll now be hiking above and parallel with the river. The treetops on your left are rooted in ground just a few feet from the river. At your feet, there are plenty of shrubs to be found, such as leadplant, which is tolerant of hot, dry conditions. After passing a trail junction on the right, you'll note some gullies to the left. These are erosive features, carved by water over the millennia since the last glacier receded. Little bluestem grass and blazing star grace the prairie near here.

By now you'll have noticed little mounds of freshly dug soil about the size of garbage can lids. Examine them closely and try to figure out what they are. There is no visible hole in the ground, and they don't seem hollow. There are no tracks on them, even though the dirt is very fresh. An easy answer would be that they're the work of aliens. But no, they're caused by pocket gophers as they push soil up and away from their burrows. The little critters never pop up above the soil, always remaining underground.

As you continue, you'll notice a house off to the left. This is a private residence. Walk across its driveway and loop around the house, at a distance of several hundred feet. You'll know you're near the river and another bridge when the trail starts downward and traverses several ridges. In late summer and early fall, you'll see an expansive silvery stand of prairie sage on the left as you drop down these ridges to the river. Make sure you drag your hand across one of these plants and then smell your fingers. Wow, no Thanksgiving turkey dressing ever exuded a more sagelike aroma!

The next 1,000 feet or so of trail are very near the river and often quite wet. The vegetation is thick and lush. Red-twig dogwood dominate the understory and elm reach for sunlight. Up on the high ground to your right is the Moorhead State University Regional Science Center. Look for signs of student projects, such as nature trail

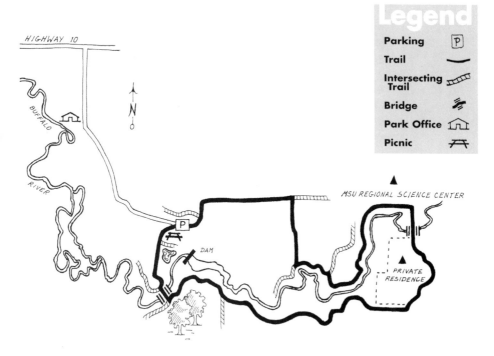

plant identification tags, around you in the woods and in the prairie up ahead. These change with the semester and the students, and they can be very interesting and informative. Keep bearing left along the river bank. Oftentimes there are unofficial trails that lead to the right, up the hillside, to the science center.

A wood post marks the junction of the Prairie Smoke Trail, which you should take to the right. A steep, short climb takes you out of the river bottom and back to the prairie. In the fall, drifts of yellow goldenrod and purple-hued big bluestem paint a colorful portrait. Indeed, you'll walk through an immense expanse of big bluestem, its 5- to 6-foot-tall stalks bearing seed in a familiar "turkey foot" fashion. When you can see over the bluestem as you walk, note the raised train tracks on the horizon. Back in 1906, the Northern Pacific Railroad embarked on a project to raise the rail bed, thereby easing the pull for heavily loaded trains. Some of the fill for the bed came from an area within the park, which you will walk by shortly.

When you reach the intersection with Wide Sky Trail, turn left. You are now a quarter mile from the river, the farthest from it you'll get on this walk. Note that the topography here is flat, save for the raised rail bed. You are walking on the bed of Glacial Lake Agassiz, which is the biggest glacial lake formed in Minnesota during the latest Wisconsin glacial period. Back then, the lake covered 20 percent of Minnesota and a large part of North Dakota, southern Manitoba, and Ontario. The lake is named after Louis Agassiz, one of the first geologists to advance the idea that glaciers helped shape our landscape.

On a less grand scale, note that there is alfalfa growing along the Wide Sky Trail here. This entire area north of the river is restored prairie. The fact that alfalfa still grows here, despite many efforts to eradicate it, speaks to this nonnative plant's tenacity.

When you reach the asphalt pavement, you'll walk through the area that provided fill for the rail bed. Stroll down the pavement for a few hundred yards and then stay left on a dirt road that heads back down to the river bottom and the parking area where you started this hike.

21

Kame and Kettle Walk
Glacial Lakes State Park

Distance: 5 miles

Time: 2 to 3 hours

Path: Mostly grass or, more correctly, prairie plants, including grasses that have been mowed. Near the top of some of the steeper kames, the path has worn down to dirt, exposing an intriguing mix of sand, gravel, and larger rocks that comprises glacial till. Low, moist places along the trail are sometimes uneven, horses' hooves having punched 3-inch-deep depressions into the soft mud. The horses have left other evidence of their passing, so be careful where you step. Most intersections are marked with wood posts. There are also occasional map boards at critical junctions.

Directions: From Starbuck, which is approximately 24 miles southwest of Alexandria, take County Highway 29 south for 3.5 miles to County Highway 41. Go south for 2 miles to the park entrance on the left. A state park sticker is required.

Contact: Glacial Lakes State Park, 25022 County Road 41, Starbuck, MN 56381; (320) 239-2860.

Highlights: There's a lot of variety on this walk, with a trail winding over kame tops, between blue kettle lakes, and through native prairie plants.

There are several excellent hikes through this area that begin at various points within the park. Start this hike at the Trail Center parking lot, which is nestled in a glacial valley. You'll begin the walk by heading to the southwest from the south end of the lot. The trail climbs out of the valley and joins a cross trail near a small copse of trees sheltering two outhouses. The large cottonwood that dominates the copse has a diameter of 4 feet and is the biggest tree you'll see on this hike. It undoubtedly offers pleasant shade to outhouse users on hot summer afternoons. Turn left at the trail junction and continue along a dry ridge that runs 10 feet above a cattail marsh on the right. Out in the distance, about a mile away on the next ridge top, silos and spruce spires vie for your attention.

At this point, prairie plants crunch under your boots. At first, crushing and bruising clumps of little bluestem grass and various asters is disconcerting. Yet this area gets mowed regularly, and somebody in authority has sanctioned this as the official path, so try to get over your queasiness and hike on. You'll feel better as you let the expansiveness of the place take over your senses. In addition to the little bluestem, you'll soon see, off to the left, wind-driven waves of big bluestem ripple on a distant hillside. A cattail marsh, along with some open water, cover a large area at the bottom of the mowed ridge top. Ducks breed here in the spring, and flights of them fill the air at dawn and dusk in the fall.

As you pass a trail junction on the left, continue straight. A cone-shaped kame stand out ahead. The mowed trail makes a slightly curved line up its side. As you begin your ascent, look off to the right. You'll see, near the edge of the marsh, about 40 yards away, a single tree. It's small, only about 15 feet tall. In the spring, fragrant white blossoms draw your attention; in late summer, brilliant red fruit about an inch in diameter grab your eye. This is a hawthorn, one of a few that dot this prairie.

As you climb the kame, note the exposed soil near the top. It is composed of small rocks, lots of sand, and a coarse mixture of earth, all of which was carried by meltwater as it drained through a gigantic glacier 10,000 years ago, eventually creating the hill you're on.

From the kame top you have a commanding view of the area. Count each body of blue water that you can see. (There are about 15.) Several of these are actually one body of water: the rolling topography breaks them apart, making much of the open water invisible from this vantage point. Imagine the area as it must have been 150 years ago. There could be a thousand buffalo over the nearest ridge and you wouldn't see them.

From the junction on top of the kame, head right, down to Kettle Lake. Prairie dropseed, a grass, dominates the

COUNTY 41

MOUNTAIN LAKE

P

HORSE CAMP

KETTLE LAKE

BABY LAKE

N

Legend

Parking · P

Trail · —

Intersecting Trail

Campsite

Marsh

trail here, as does leadplant, a short fine-leafed plant whose terminal branch ends light up with iridescent blue-purple flowers in August. Although some maps show four different bodies of water along the trail on the left, recent heavy winter snows and abundant spring moisture have raised water levels enough so that all the small lakes have become one large body of water. Four big barkless cottonwoods stand as sad testament to the high water, their thick and naked trunks rising out of the lake, near its edge.

Yet a profusion of new vegetation jostles for space in the 5 to 20 feet between the trail and the lake. A 10-foot-tall box elder is smothered by Virginia creeper and grapevines, with prairie plants carpeting the area underneath. One huge Solomon seal, an unexpected inhabitant, sticks its graceful leaflets out from under the thicket.

As you loop around the southeast end of the water, look up and to the right and you'll see seven distinct humps along the hillside. These may be the result of glacial meltwater running off the top of the hill, or perhaps they are erosive features caused by more modern water. The trail passes below them for the next couple of hundred yards before it leads you away from Kettle Lake. As it does, you'll note a solitary tree, about 20 feet tall, off to the left. This bur oak, the first that you'll see on this walk, looks lonely out there. But if you want to see more, take a right on the spur trail several hundred yards ahead that leads to Baby Lake. At first hidden by the rolling hills, the lake and its shoreline forest will pop into view shortly after you head down this trail. Find the path that leads through the forest to the lakeshore; from there you can see the prairie shoreline on the opposite side. You'll be standing in the shade of more big old bur oaks while gazing across at the nakedness of the prairie, and the contrast is striking.

From the lake, hike back down the spur trail and turn right. This path will take you back to the kame top you were on before. Go right at the intersection on the top. The trail will dip down near an area on the right that looks as if it had been a small lake that is now filled in with sediment. The trail then climbs up and back down another kame. Raspberry canes tangle with each other and cover a quarter of an acre on the left. Keep to the left, avoiding the two trail junctions that form a loop out and over yet another kame, and you'll approach a large woods, filled mostly with oak. A buffer of staghorn sumac several hundred feet wide sprouts from the prairie in the shelter of this forest. Perhaps park officials haven't been able to burn this area near the woods as intensely and hence successfully as other areas in the park.

Loop around in front of the woods and hike to the next trail junction, where you'll turn right; the parking area is about a half mile away.

Lower and Upper Cliffline and Upper Mound Trails
Blue Mounds State Park

Distance: 5 miles

Time: 2 to 3 hours

Path: Easy to follow, most of it on a surface of mowed prairie, with one moderately strenuous, although not technically difficult, climb up a fault in the 90-foot-high rock face.

Directions: From the intersection of Interstate 90 and Highway 75 south of Luverne, take 75 north 5.5 miles to County Highway 20. Turn right and go about 1 mile to the park entrance. Drive into the park as far as you can and park at the Lower Mound Lake beach parking area.

Contact: Blue Mounds State Park, RR 1, Box 52, Luverne, MN 56156- 9610; (507)283-1307.

Highlights: The park offers many outstanding sights and sounds. Near the highest point of the gently sloping mound you can see the horizon in all directions 360 degrees! Walk along the base of the 90-foot-tall quartzite cliffs and marvel at the color and sheerness of the rock. View the prairie atop the mound in late June and see yellow prickly pear catus flowers bloom amid pale blue spiderwort. Explore the 1,250-foot-long Stonehenge-type rock line that marks the spring and fall equinox. Or listen to the mating calls of the bobolink and western meadowlark in the spring. Plus, there's the 40 to 50 head of semiwild buffalo that roam a large fenced area in the park.

The giant mound that gave this park its name is visible from Highway 75 as you drive north out of Luverne. Under proper lighting conditions (and perhaps during some seasons more than others), the mound, which rises gently from left to right, takes on a blue hue. In any light, the mound is an impressive treeless expanse of original prairie sod that presages your entrance into the park and a wonderful hike.

From the parking area, hike down a cement ramp past the bathhouse to a map board. Continue along the lake, on the trail closest to it. Head toward the dam, then turn right up the wide old spillway to another map board. Begin walking the Lower Cliffline Trail, strewn with large boulders that have fallen from the cliff. On the left is a vast expanse of flatland: the prairie that is part of the park extends only a quarter mile or so, then cultivated fields stretch beyond. Plants along the trail here include prairie rose, milkweed, wolfberry, and horsetail.

You'll soon arrive at five bur oak standing near the cliff face, providing relief and perspective to the sheer walls. Continue on between two huge old oaks near the base of the cliff, and you'll spot a crevice that cuts cleanly through the cliff from the top almost to the bottom. You'll pass a thicket of small plum trees and a concave jog in the cliff face, from which enormous boulders have tumbled, cluttering the path and providing protected niches for more plums and oaks and box elder trees. Poison ivy also enjoys this protection, so watch for it.

You'll reach another recession in the cliff face where a sign marks the "One Mile Loop," with an arrow pointing into and up the concave recession. You'll want to take the trail that angles left, away from the rock face. This route takes you to a mowed roadlike path that parallels the cliff line several hundred feet from it. From here you can get a great view of the cliff and the wonderful bur oak scattered along its base.

In a couple of hundred yards, follow the mowed path leading directly back to the cliff face and something called the Mini Fortress area. Huge boulders have tumbled down off the cliff to form a jumble of bare rock. Clamber over them if you'd like and gaze out at the broad plain stretching east.

Hike back out to the wide mowed path and continue south, to the right. Slowly, the path takes you back toward the cliff face. As you get closer to it, you'll note that no trees or other woody vegetation block your view of the cliff face. Park personnel have cleared them away in an attempt to restore how the area probably looked before Europeans altered this prairie landscape with plows and domesticated animals. It's also a good place to examine the rock that forms the cliff and underlies the entire mound.

By now you should have noticed that the color of the rock varies from a light pink to red to a dusty purple. The basic coloring is caused by iron oxide, iron that's been exposed to air and water and is better known as rust. Sometimes the rock even looks blue-green. This is caused by lichen (a symbiotic combination of algae and fungus) growing on the rock.

Geologists call this rock Sioux quartzite. Its formation began over a billion and a half years ago as sand was deposited on the bottom of a vast sea. With time and more sand and water, sandstone was formed; then, with even more time and sediment and some chemical reactions, this sandstone turned into the Sioux quartzite in front of you.

When you've examined enough rock, continue up the trail that, when reunited with the cliff base, quickly turns upward and into the cliff. It's a short but steep climb over large rocks to the top of the cliff you've been hiking beneath for the last mile. At the top, settle into a bench and take in the fine view of the countryside to the east. You'll see clusters of trees protecting farmland from the relentless west and northwest winds, and a few scattered trees mark low, small, untilled areas. The rest of the terrain reflects the geometry of cultivated 40s, 80s, and 160s: squares and rectangles measured in acres and bisected by byways every 5,080 feet.

Look left along the edge of the cliff for another unique view from the bench. Note that the tops of all the bigger bur oak growing at the base of the cliff protrude above the cliff. They look odd, like trunkless trees or giant bushes somehow hanging in thin air.

When you're rested, head down the path, now called the Upper Cliffline Trail. From the bench, you'll want to go right; but from the orientation you had when you climbing the cliff, go left. In about a quarter mile, you'll come to a gigantic bowl-shaped depression in the cliff face that doesn't look natural and it isn't. The real trail takes you around this bowl at a safe distance from its rim, while an unofficial but often-used trail traces the rim. Both lead you to the bowl's south-west edge and a signboard. It says that from 1919 until 1931 this area was a quarry from which as many as 600 tons of rock were removed each day. Much of it was crushed on site before being hauled away and later mixed with cement for various building projects.

Another quarter mile down the trail, you'll arrive at the Blue Mounds Rock Alignment. This is an odd linear arrangement of surface-collected quartzite 1,250 feet long. What makes it strange is its east-west orientation and the fact that on the first day of spring and of fall, the equinoxes, the sun rises and sets in perfect alignment with each end of this rock line. No one knows who arranged the stone in this fashion or when it was done.

Another 150 yards down the trail is the park's interpretive center. Built as a private residence in 1960, the center today provides visitors with information about the area and the park. It's worth a look because it was built right into the mound and constructed out of Sioux quartzite quarried on site.

The rest of this hike is across the top of the mound. Head back uphill from the interpretive center past where the Upper Cliffline Trail ends, to a sign that points you down a short spur trail to Eagle Rock. From the rock, at 1,730 feet above sea level, you can look down on the town of Luverne about 4 miles south and 300 feet closer to sea level. On your way back up the spur trail to the main trail, note the expanses of big bluestem and side-oats grama, both native prairie grasses. When you get to the next map board, turn right onto the Upper Mound Trail.

You'll now cross the top of the great blue mound. Big hunks of rock lie flat, exposed, stripped of soil, and covered with strangely delicate and intricately shaped lichen. The next signboard, titled Prairie Vista, is adjacent to such an outcrop. It was here, in June 1838, that Joseph Nicollet, an early French explorer, took in the view and marveled at the color of the vast expanse of grasses and prairie plants before him. Now it's your turn. There are very few places on land where the distant curve of the earth is all that limits your view. That's Iowa farmland you see to the south and South Dakota to the west.

The rest of this hike, more than a mile, is essentially all downhill, 200 feet downhill! About 150 feet from the Prairie Vista is a map board at a trail junction. Go left here to the next trail junction, which will be with the Lower Mound Trail. If it's early summer, you'll be surrounded by lots of blooming prairie plants, such as whorled milkweed, Canada anemone, Culver's root, and the pink and lavender blooms of prairie phlox. When you reach the map board at the Lower Mound Trail junction, go right.

You'll soon see the buffalo range, which is enclosed by a tall, sturdy fence, where the trail jogs right, then left, and hugs the fence all the way back to the parking lot. Look for the huge animals. And, as the sign near their enclosure warns, "Don't tease the buffalo."

Legend

Parking	P
Trail	—
Intersecting Trail	
Park Office	
Bench	
View	

75

Hikes into History

Cut Foot Sioux/ Simpson Creek Trail
Chippewa National Forest

Distance: 6 miles

Time: 3 hours

Path: Varied, from woodland grasses to wet muck in the cedar swamp. Although the trail is well marked, with map boards at most inter-sections, you should carry a map. There are many intersecting trails along the path; the wrong one will take you miles out of your way.

Directions: From the intersection of Highways 2 and 46 in Deer River, take Highway 46 northwest 17 miles to the Cut Foot Sioux visitor center. This is where the hike ends, and since it is a long hike, you may want to either arrange for transportation back to the starting point or drop a vehicle here and proceed to the start. Mountain bikes are permitted on the trail, so leaving a bike here would be an option. Pick up a map and other information at the visitor center, then proceed back up Highway 46 about 5 miles north to County Road 33. Go west (left) on 33 about 5 miles to the parking area for the East Seelye Bay campground.

Contact: Chippewa National Forest, Deer River Ranger District, Box 308, Deer River, MN 56636; (218)246-2123.

Highlights: There is lots of history in the area, including the way the Cut Foot Sioux Lake acquired its name. The forest itself has a colorful his-tory, one of fires and logging and some uncut timbers.

This hike is in a remote area and it's long, two reasons for you to carry a compass and a few supplies in case there's a problem.

Since you'll leave your vehicle in a parking area that boarders Cut Foot Sioux Lake, stroll over to the water's edge and take a look. It is a wild North Woods scene: big water, with islands in the distance, large expanses of emergent vegetation, either bur reed or wild rice, and a few cottages and resorts breaking an otherwise tree-covered shoreline.

You may wonder how the lake and, later, the trail, got the name Cut Foot Sioux. According to Ojibwa legend, a skirmish broke out between two small war parties of Chippewa and Sioux. Eventually, the

Chippewa chased the Sioux across the lake. Upon reaching shore, the Sioux hoisted their canoe on their backs and began running down a portage trail. When the Chippewa arrived, they found the body of a mortally wounded Sioux lying on the ground. He had no feet, these apparently having been cut or frozen off sometime before. After that encounter, the lake became known as Cut Foot Sioux.

The trailhead is across the road from the lake. The trail traces a path near a steep embankment, down to what seems a back bay of Cut Foot Sioux Lake, but which is sometimes called Dry Creek Lake. Verdant gray twig dogwood line the trail, reaching over 15 feet high. The trail loops back out to County Road 33 and briefly joins the road in crossing a wetland on the edge of the lake. Follow the road until the trail reenters the woods on the right, just past the wetland, then parallels the road. You'll then cross the driveway for Eagle Nest Lodge. You may see trash strewn on or near the trail for several hundred feet past the driveway. This is not the result of careless humans tossing out garbage but of hungry black bears raiding a Dumpster on the right side of the trail. Note the electrified fencing around it. These bears must really be persistent.

Soon afterwards, the trail enters a small campground on the shore of Cut Foot Sioux Lake. This is part of Eagle Nest Lodge. Walk through the campground clearing and you'll reenter the trail. Soon you'll see more water on the left, a little lake that is quickly filling up with vegetation, a process called eutrophication.

Now you'll climb a bit onto higher, dryer ground, where red and white pine abound. There are some large white pine here, and you'll also get your last good view of Cut Foot Sioux Lake to the right. The trail then angles away from the two lakes and enters a vast red pine grove, crosses Forest Road 2230, and continues up and down glacial hills forested with red pine.

After a junction with a spur road off of Forest Road 2230, the red pine grove temporarily ends and the trail dips down into a low area. There's a junction just ahead, marked with a post and a sign with a big "D" on it. There are several hundred acres of 10- to 15-foot-tall planted red pine beyond the sign. Turn right at the junction. The planted pine will be on your left. The trail here is relatively straight. And look out for bears. They love to feast on the berries that grow in the open areas among the red pine.

At the next junction, marked "E," keep right but first take note of the big white pine just behind the trail marker. The trail beyond it becomes straight again and has the straight, slightly raised feel of an old railroad grade.

The next junction is important: a wrong turn takes you miles out of your way. The junction letter on the ski-trail map is "F," but there may not be a letter on the map post. Bear left and stay left. You'll hike

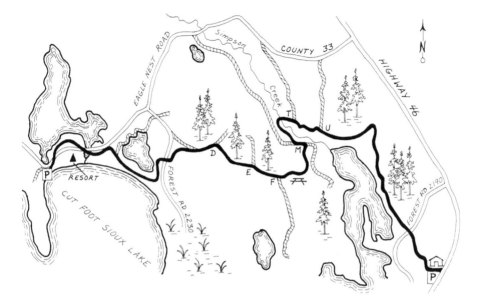

Parking	P
Trail	—
Intersecting Trail	
Park Office	
Picnic	
Marsh	

up a little knoll; and if you see a picnic table, you're on the right track, but stay left. A large area of clear-cut forest will be visible on the right soon after the picnic table. Then you'll make a long, gradual climb up the steepest hill you've encountered so far on the hike. And you'll still be surrounded by red pine.

At the next junction, unlettered on the map, the trail you're on makes a T with another trail that runs along on top of an esker. An esker is a glacial formation created when creeks run under glaciers and deposit sand and gravel, thus raising the ground level and creating a long, sinuous ridge. Go left on the esker and within 50 yards turn right at junction "M." You'll encounter two downhill pitches here, taking you to a wooden bridge over Simpson Creek, named for a logger who contracted to remove most of the virgin timber from the region back in 1907.

From the wooden bridge, you can see the creek bed: a quarter-mile-wide break in the forest canopy, dotted with alder and grasses. Across the creek you'll see a stretch of dead white pine in the low-lying area. It's likely that a flood caused by a beaver dam killed the trees. You'll then ascend on a pine needle-covered path and reach junction "T." Continue straight (slightly right) to junction "U," where you'll make another right turn.

Until now, most of this hike has been among various red and white pine groves, which were established after fires around the turn of the century. Now you'll be entering a different type of grove, one that's relatively rare today. Here the ground is wetter and the forest darker. Balsam fir and spruce have replaced the pine. Then you'll begin to see white cedar, which at first appear scattered and small, but then become more closely bunched and bigger in size. Look for the cedar stump in the middle of the trail. It has more than 100 growth rings, making the tree it was once part of over 100 years old. And there are several cedar near the stump that are twice as big as the stump tree!

The trail climbs out of the cedar swamp and continues down the side of an arm of Cut Foot Sioux Lake, which you can see as you approach Forest Road 2190. Linger for a while and watch for moose in the marshland around the lake. When you cross the road you are almost back to the visitor center. Go left at the black topped path and you'll finish this hike in the visitor center parking lot.

Homestead Trail
Hayes Lake State Park

Distance: 2.5 miles

Time: 1.5 hours

Path: This is an easy trek, nearly all of it on level surfaces. The path begins as a mowed-grass road, 16 feet wide, then narrows to a 4- to 6-foot-wide swath. There are numbered stations that correspond to descriptions in a brochure available at the park office.

Directions: From the intersection of Highways 89, 11, and 310 in Roseau, take 89 south approximately 14.5 miles to County Highway 4. Go east on County 4 for 8 miles to the park entrance on the right.

Contact: Hayes Lake State Park, 48990 County Road 4, Roseau, MN 56751; (218)425-7504.

Highlights: With a little imagination, this is a hike back in time, to when a family did the arduous work of clearing trees, plowing root-riddled ground, and constructing a home. You can sit under the flowering crab trees they planted and partake some of the fragrance and beauty, thanks to these hard-working folks.

Hayes Lake State Park is in the running for the most remote state park in Minnesota. On the drive here, you'll observe an odd mix of northern wetland trees, such as black spruce and tamarack, yet there are acres of farm fields set amid a very flat landscape. Once in the park, the forest engulfs you, leaving no doubt about where you are: up north . . . far up north. Yet this forest is a bit odd too. But more about that later.

Start this wonderful walk from anywhere near the parking area at the dam. Follow the road back from the parking area and turn left when you reach a junction. You'll be hiking down a sandy, grass-covered road that once provided access to a fire tower and small homestead. The road was built in the early 1900s and closed in 1967.

The road cuts through a forest that is remarkable for its abundance of many old and large specimens of jack pine. Jack pine grow on sandy, often dry soils; they also do well in areas where fires have traditionally swept the landscape. Some of their seeds are sequestered in cones that open and scatter their contents only when temperatures

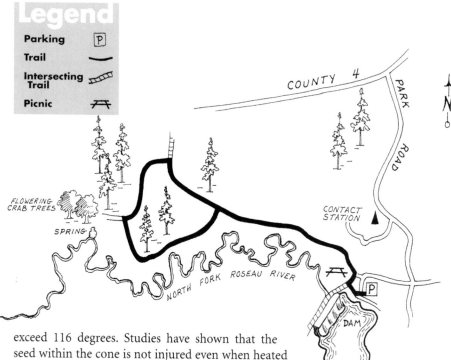

Legend

Parking   P

Trail

Intersecting Trail

Picnic

COUNTY 4

PARK ROAD

N

FLOWERING CRAB TREES

SPRING

CONTACT STATION

NORTH FORK ROSEAU RIVER

P

DAM

exceed 116 degrees. Studies have shown that the seed within the cone is not injured even when heated to 1,300 degrees for a couple of seconds, or to 600 degrees for up to 60 seconds!

As you walk the old road, notice that different moisture-loving plants grow along the ditch, visible on the roadside. One wetland plant, speckled alder, is seen often. Sun-loving woodland flowers such as aster and goldenrod also grow along the road's edge, where both moisture and sunlight are more available.

When you reach a junction, bear left. The old fire tower is visible straight ahead, as are remnants of the foundations of several old forestry buildings. As you continue walking, just south of the tower on the left side of the trail, you'll see a small building that is still intact. Apparently this lowly outhouse had nothing worth scavenging and was left in place

Station number 5 will soon appear on the right. It is the location of what was once the Pine Needle Inn, built in 1929 by some local settlers whose homesteads you'll pass soon. There isn't much left of the old inn, save some hunks of wood and pieces of unidentifiable iron.

The pleasant forest path continues and gradually passes into an old field, cleared and farmed by the folks whose homestead you'll see ahead. The field is covered with grasses and pimpled with small islands of jack pine, white spruce, and poplar. These open-grown trees, especially the pine and spruce, look short and fat compared to their tall and svelte forest-grown cousins.

You'll then reach an intersection where the mowed path leads right and left. Take the right path about 100 feet to station number 6, where you'll find the remains of the Alva and Signe Hendershot homestead, which was established in the fall of 1910. There is not much left now, save for a few living reminders that people once settled here. Just across the mowed path from the 6 marker are two such reminders: a mock orange shrub and a thicket of Siberian pea shrubs. These do not grow here naturally; they were undoubtedly planted by the homesteaders. Just a bit farther toward the forest edge and river, you'll see the beginning of a ravine at the edge of the woods. This was location of a spring from which the homesteaders got their water. On the field side of the ravine, you can see two large flowering crab trees, which no doubt were also planted by the homesteaders.

Trace your path back to the junction and continue right. You'll first pass a pile of old farm machinery on the left, then see a clump of small trees to the right, at the woods' edge. These are balsam poplar, which spread via their roots; they are on their way to taking over the field.

The trail will then reenter the jack pine woods and soon pass two grave sites encompassed, incongruously, by a chain-link fence. These are the burial sites of relatives of the homesteaders whose shrubs and trees you just saw. See if you can read the dates on the plaques placed by park personnel above the graves. Another grave, visible a bit farther down the trail at the edge of the river valley, is marked by its original headstone, placed there in 1912. The trail hugs the edge of the valley for the next several hundred feet to marker number 10, which is where J. D. Hendershot, a relative of Alva's, had his homestead. Visible to the right of the marker is an old root cellar that being filled up with trees.

The trail then winds around following the high ground, near the edge of the valley and within 100 yards of this last homestead, eventually reconnecting with the road on which you walked out here. Turn right and head back into today.

Ogechie Lake Hike
Mille Lacs Kathio State Park

Distance: 2 miles

Time: 1 hour

Path: The path is covered with mowed grass; a few steep hills come into play on the last third of the hike. The two archaeological sites are mowed.

Directions: From the intersection of Highway 169 and County Highway 26 on the southwest shore of Mille Lacs, take 26 for 1 mile south to the park entrance. Then take the park road to the Ogechie Lake campground and park your vehicle in the area provided.

Contact: Mille Lacs Kathio State Park, 15066 Kathio State Park Road, Onamia, MN 56359; (320)532-3523.

Highlights: This trek takes you back hundreds of years, to a time when people hunted and gathered their food. Today, the remains of an old Indian settlement and a homestead established later by whites provide a glimpse of people who struggled to survive in a harsh environment.

Follow the fence and the signs from the parking area to an open patch of mowed grass leading to a peninsula that juts into Ogechie Lake. This area is the site of an Mdewakanton Dakota (Sioux) settlement, which dates as far back as 1100 and seems to have vanished around 1750. Archaeologists have studied the site intensively in the 1960s and 1970s. What they tell us is fascinating.

First, you'll notice wooden posts a foot high, set in concrete bases, that form a rectangle out onto the peninsula. These mark the site of a former perimeter wall of logs, set on end and buried in the ground. At least toward the end of its occupation by the Dakota, this was a fortified settlement. The Dakota's summer houses, rectangular structures covered by gabled roofs and fashioned from ash or elm poles, with elm bark for covering, were located within these log walls. Their winter quarters, whose floors were excavated below ground level, were located outside the walls, just to the left of the present-day post markers, at the edge of the cleared land.

Along the lakeshore, to the right, archaeologists have found three separate middens, places where the occupants of the settlement

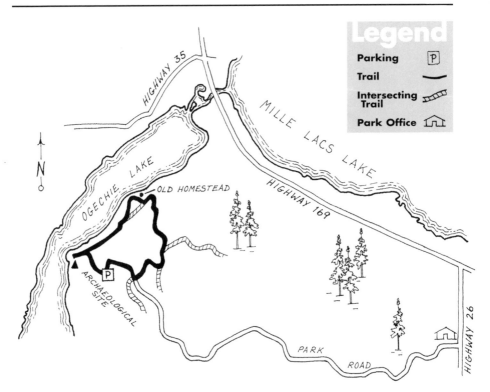

dumped their refuse. A detailed study of the middens shows that wild rice was a staple. From an analysis of various bones found in them, archaeologists also determined the type (and percentage) of animals that the early Dakota consumed: white-tailed deer, 28%; bear, beaver, and other small mammals, 20%; elk, 15%; fish, 4%; waterfowl, 3%; and bison, 30%. Since it is thought that the nearest bison roamed hundreds of miles to the south and west, these hunters must have traveled long distances to secure food. Indeed, Father Louis Hennepin, who visited the area in 1680, described such hunting parties.

Today the lakeshore is a riot of shrubs and grasses trying to dominate one another. From dry ground out to the water's edge runs a seven-foot strip of wetland full of nannyberry, bergamot, roses, raspberry, cow parsnip, and even a few Michigan lilies, bright orange flowers that blaze in the summer sun.

Don't leave the peninsula without reflecting on what existence must have been like for these early inhabitants and how remarkable their lives must have been. This is a magical place, a time machine that, aided by your imagination, can carry you back hundreds of years.

When you're ready, continue the hike by heading back up to the parking area and turning left. You'll quickly be on a grassy roadlike trail headed for your next encounter with the past. The lakeshore will be close by on the left. Watch for the only opening in the shoreline vegetation along here that gives you a glimpse of the lake's other shore. Numerous waterfowl are common here, so look for them on the lake.

The trail then turns toward the lake and takes you out onto another peninsula, where another old Dakota settlement site was located. The first site is visible from the second.

Next, head up a gravel ramp to higher ground and you'll enter a clearing, the site of an immigrant's homestead dating back to the mid- to late-1800s. Near the middle of the clearing, note the depression in the ground and the large stones it contains, remnants of the home's foundation. A worn sloping path that leads into the hole from the south is thought to have been the entrance to the root cellar under the home. To the south of the foundation is a row of lilac bushes, obvious ancestors of those cultivated by the homesteaders.

Generally, homesteading in the region didn't work out. The various soils here are poor and unsuited to growing crops. The weather is harsh. An early freeze killed a season's worth of food production, or a long drought did the same. Indeed, the dust bowl days of the 1930's ended many an attempt to farm the area. The land reverted back to the government, and now has become a place for everyone.

Unless you want to retrace your path here, the trail back to the starting point is a mowed path that leaves the clearing next to a giant white spruce, possibly rescued from loggers over the years because it was part of the homestead. At over 9 feet in circumference, it's one of the largest white spruce in the state or the country. You'll walk through some shrubby hazel, small white pine, and bur oak, then under a power line. Here, the trail begins its loop back toward the parking area and away from the lake.

The terrain on the rest of the walk is very different from the flat lakefront path that brought you to this point. There are lots of short, steep hills, typical of glacial topography. At the first junction you'll want to bear right. Going left will take you on a very long hike through the interior of the park. At the next junction turn right again. You'll see a "Most Difficult" cross-country-skiing sign on a post near the junction. The trail becomes narrow here, and even steeper. After climbing two "nose-to-toes" hills, you'll reach the park road. Turn right the parking area is close by.

Mazomani's Prairie Hike
Upper Sioux Agency State Park

Distance: 1 mile

Time: 1 hour

Path: The surface is mostly grass, with some asphalt where it runs along the park road. There are no signs that mark this walk.

Directions: From the intersection of Highways 23 and 67 in Granite Falls, take 67 southeast 8 miles along the Minnesota River to the park entrance on the left.

Contact: Upper Sioux Agency State Park, Route 2, Box 92, Granite Falls, MN 56241; (320)564-4777.

Highlights: The view of the Minnesota River valley and of its confluence with the Yellow Medicine River is unbeatable. Yet the area saw terrible sadness and injustice, as you'll learn from reading the story of Mazomani described in the park's literature.

Start your walk at the east end of the park road, where a Minnesota Historical Society metal sign stands on the bluff near an overlook. First, let yourself experience the loveliness of the area. Watch for raptors soaring over the confluence of the Minnesota and Yellow Medicine Rivers before you. Mingle yourself with the place. Then read the sign. It tells the poignant story of Mazomani, a Dakota man who was shot by American soldiers, presumably while carrying a white flag of truce, in 1862. His death came near the end of a month-long rebellion by the Dakota, who had been confined to a long, narrow band of land along the Minnesota. Mazomani's descendants still live in the area.

After reading the sign, walk east, away from the road. You'll find a path that leads out onto a bluff top prairie. It is said that Mazomani is buried on this bluff, overlooking the land he loved. Depending on the season, you'll see a tapestry of native flowers: blazing star, pasque flower, several types of goldenrod, penstemon, prairie sage, coneflower, puccoon, and aster. Native grasses growing here include big and little bluestem, Indian grass, side-oats grama, and needle grass.

Amid the prairie plants are lots of old stumps. These are from juniper and sumac, two prairie invaders that have been cut back. If

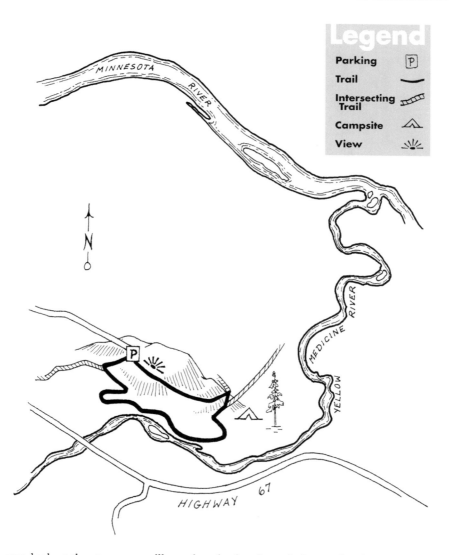

you look at the stumps, you'll see that they're charred, the result of fires set here to discourage any further colonization by these unwanted woody plants.

When you come to a spot where the trail drops off the bluff, stop for a moment and look around. The view is enormous. Below, along the bluff, is the Minnesota River Valley. Home to a profusion of wildlife, the river stretches from near the boarder with South Dakota all the way to its meeting with the Mississippi just south of the Twin Cities. It's not unusual to spot a bald eagle soaring overhead.

Look toward the Yellow Medicine River and the campground east and south of you; that's where you're headed. You'll then begin to descend the bluff as the trail snakes its way through more sumac stumps. Turn right at the next two trail junctions and wind down to the road. Cross the road and head for a white pine and the campground beyond, across an open field. This field and, indeed, the entire peninsula near the confluence of the two rivers, have been used as a seasonal encampment for centuries. Archeologists tell us that the area has been occupied for 8,000 years!

As you continue, you'll walk to the edge of a minibluff, where the high ground ends before you reach the campground. As you stand next to the white pine, you'll see another tree, this one an apple planted by the folks whose farmstead this was years ago.

Make your way back to the road and walk a short distance to a sign on the right, which announces "Walk-in Campsites." Take this trail to the right until you reach the first junction. Then go left and follow this trail past sites 2, 3, and 4. The Yellow Medicine River is close by on your left. The bass fishing is good here. There are some large eastern cottonwood trees on the opposite bank.

The trail then climbs back up to the road, crosses it, and loops along a hillside. This hillside shows evidence of having been burned, another attempt to foster the growth of native plants. The path goes back down to the road and along it, then dives right into a meadow. This too was the site of an old farmstead. Note the Siberian elm trees scattered across the meadow, the progeny of ones planted by the homesteaders. They seem out of place here and they often overwhelm some of our native plants; park personnel are working to eliminate them.

The trail switches back as it begins a climb up an old farmstead road back to the top of the bluff where you began this walk. Note the lilacs growing at the base of the hill. When you reach the top 200 feet from where you began the ascent turn right at the junction and you'll see the parking lot in the distance.

Zumbro Hill Cemetery Hike
Forestville State Park

Distance: 1 mile

Time: 1 hour

Path: Composed of crushed gravel and dirt, and easy to follow. The trail is almost entirely uphill on the way to the cemetery, the focal point of this walk.

Directions: From Preston take Highway 16 about 12 miles west to County Highway 5. Go left(south)on County 5 for 4 miles to County Highway 12. Take County 12 left(east) for 2 miles to the park entrance. Once into the park, bear left past the information station and go past the town of Forestville, to a small parking area on the left, near several rows of white pine.

Contact: Forestville State Park, Route 2, Box 128, Preston, MN 55965; (507)352-5111.

Highlights: Forestville State Park is diverse. Unique because of its preservation and restoration of the nineteenth-century town of Forestville, it also boasts a lovely hardwood forest carpeted with wildflowers in the spring. This walk focuses on one of the park's historic sites: the cemetery where the town's pioneers are buried.

As you hike up the wide path that begins this walk, imagine a funeral cortege from the 1860s, with a horse pulling a cart bearing a wooden casket, followed by a line of mourners. But before you get into the mood, visit what's left of the Forestville Grade School, built in 1879 and 1880; it's located just off to the right of the trail as you head away from the road. Some concrete steps lead up to a rectangular hole in the ground, inside of which are the remnants of the school: a few chunks of stone and some pieces of lumber. The most striking feature is a poplar tree, more than 30 years old and about 60 feet high, that stands at the center.

Back on the graveled trail, you'll climb a few hundred feet to a signboard that tells of a brickyard that once operated here. Established in 1856 by John Gill, the facility manufactured bricks using clay from the site and water that flowed from hillside springs. If you look behind the signboard, you'll see the area where the springs still moisten the ground. On the other side of the trail, across from the signboard, you can see that the topography is uneven, with small, 2-

to 4-foot-high ridges running down the hillside. These are what's left of the clay excavations.

The trail continues uphill and makes a right turn where a sign with an arrow points to Pioneer Cemetery. Shortly after this turn, the walk gets steep for about 100 feet. Then it levels out a bit but continues to climb. There's another right turn in about 300 yards, then another short climb, until you reach a signboard marking the cemetery boundary.

The cemetery was used from 1856 until 1899. Walk on ahead and read the inscriptions on some of the headstones, although most are so worn that they are very difficult to read. One, near the signboard, is inscribed "Christopher Brant, Born in Fayette Co Penn, Dec 17 1805, Died, Nov 8 1857."

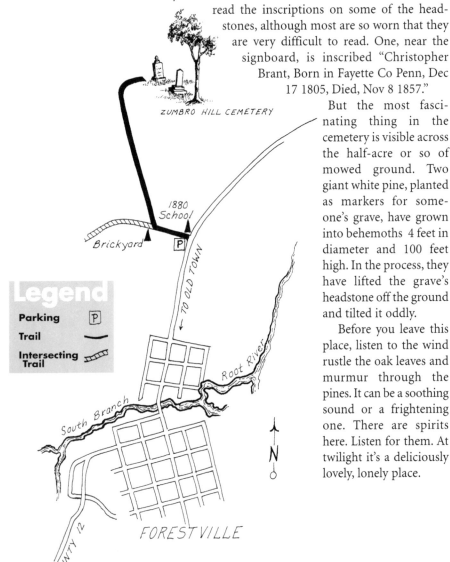

But the most fascinating thing in the cemetery is visible across the half-acre or so of mowed ground. Two giant white pine, planted as markers for someone's grave, have grown into behemoths 4 feet in diameter and 100 feet high. In the process, they have lifted the grave's headstone off the ground and tilted it oddly.

Before you leave this place, listen to the wind rustle the oak leaves and murmur through the pines. It can be a soothing sound or a frightening one. There are spirits here. Listen for them. At twilight it's a deliciously lovely, lonely place.

Strolls among Wildlife

Echo Bay Trail
Voyageurs National Park

Distance: 2 miles

Time: 1 hour

Path: This is a forest trail, likely an old logging road, that is grass covered and somewhat uneven. The area is mostly flat. The only information available on the path is on a signboard at the trailhead, a map posted at a trail junction about halfway through the hike, and a sign announcing the overlook.

Directions: From the junction of Highway 53 and County Road 122, about 25 miles southeast of International Falls, take 122 north approximately 4 miles to Northern Lights Road. Go east (right) on Northern Lights to the parking area on the left.

Contact: Voyageurs National Park, 3131 Highway 53, International Falls, MN 56649; (218)283-9821.

Highlights: This trail makes a big loop around a vast area flooded by beaver dams. There are several good views of the flooded timber, and you may encounter one of the flat-tailed, buck-toothed creatures. Wolves live here too, and chances are good you'll see prints or scat if you look hard enough. For a real thrill, hike this trail at night and let the wolves send a chill down your back with a primitive howl.

From the parking area find the signboard to the left of the cleared area; the trail begins just to the left of the sign. Nearly all the first mile of this hike is though a poplar and aspen forest, with some black ash and a few cedar mixed in. The understory is full of the usual hazelnut, ferns, and large-leafed aster. Two less common plants that abound here are both viburnums: the highbush cranberry, no relation to the lowland cranberry, and the nannyberry. The nannyberry fruits look like small dates and are said to taste like dates after they've been touched by frost.

When you reach the sign that announces the overlook, take the short spur trail to it. The overlook is really just a rock escarpment, not very high, that provides a look at a lowland full of dead trees. Even though they are the type that grow in wet areas, spruce, elm, and black ash, they couldn't endure the standing water that resulted from the work of industrious beavers. You can't see the dam that flooded the area but, rest assured, it's out there.

There is a bench at the overlook. Around it on the rocks eking out a living are some sumac, short but alive. Have a seat and see if any beavers appear down in the water beneath the dead and dying trees. If not or if you get tired of waiting, head back to the main trail and turn right. This next section of woods has more spruce and other conifers than the first part you hiked through. There are also some basswood, a tree that's near the northern edge of its range here.

At the next trail junction, there's a map board. Turn right and traverse some boards placed over a wet area; you'll be hiking down a long straight section of trail that may have been the path for an old narrow-gauge logging railroad. Black willow grow in the wet ditch on the right of the trail, and beyond that you can see more of the beaver pond filled with dead trees. Eventually the trail curves left into an

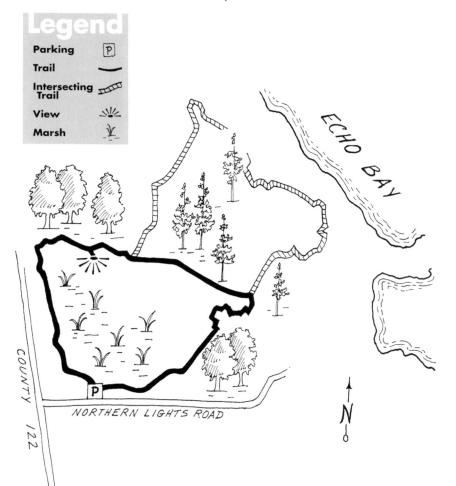

Legend

Parking   P

Trail

Intersecting Trail

View

Marsh

ECHO BAY

COUNTY 122

P

NORTHERN LIGHTS ROAD

N

opening and skirts the pond itself. You're likely to encounter ducks in the pond or at least hear them quacking nearby.

The trail then reenters the woods, which is now mostly spruce, aspen, and balsam fir. Some of the aspen bear scars from beavers who started a felling job but quit. There is also a little swamp filled with oddly canted cedar trees reaching for light. After passing close to a giant aspen over 2 feet in diameter and a couple of good-sized red pine on a slope to the left, the trail reaches another junction.

Head right across a boardwalk and a small creek. If the water isn't too high, the soft mud along here is a good place to look for wolf tracks. There is a pack that inhabits this end of the park, and the local folks will tell you they hear them howling at night.

The area flooded by beaver is still visible on the right, then you enter another cedar swamp. Two large cedar on the right must be over 150 years old. Then the trail climbs over a massive rock slab, gains about 10 feet of elevation, and enters a dryer woods, again full of aspen and balsam poplar. After passing an opening that harbors wild-flowers such as aster and goldenrod, the trail winds through a small aspen stand that is tilted about 15 degrees to the east. This must be a windy spot. From here it's only a little way to the parking area.

29
South Dark River Hiking Trail
Superior National Forest

Distance: 2.5 miles, round trip

Time: 1 hour

Path: Unmowed grass, other forest-floor plants, and litter, plus a hilly trail that at one point snakes along a high riverbank, make for a moderately difficult walk. There are also no trail markers, so it's sometimes difficult to get your bearings. Take a compass and be prepared for unexpected problems because you're a long way from anything other than woods and wild things.

Directions: From Chisholm, take Highway 73 north approximately 12 miles to County Highway 65. Go east (right) on 65 for 1.5 miles to Forest Service Road 271. Go north (left) on 271 and it's 1.75 miles to the trail's map board. Forest Service Road 271 is not maintained, so be cautious.

Contact: Superior National Forest, Laurentian Ranger District, 318 Forestry Road, Aurora, MN 55705; (218)229-3371.

Highlights: This is a hike into a remote area, free of roads and with abundant wildlife. The Dark River is twisting and slow, full of beaver dams. Although its name imparts a slightly sinister feel, it was named for its tannin-rich content, which turns the water a deep brown.

B egin your hike at the map board. You may note that the map shows a couple of loops along the trail that are not rendered on the map on the next page. We couldn't find two of the three loops, so all of them have been left out of this book.

An impressively large jack pine graces the trail about 50 feet in from the road on the left. It's dead, but its lichen-adorned branches and stubbornly clinging cones are an intriguing sight. You'll cross a snowmobile trail before the trail you are on dips into the first of several ravines. Various kinds of club moss grow in abundance along the ground here, including wolf-claw and shining and running cedar club mosses. Once the trail climbs up again, you'll note other small ground-hugging plants, including bunchberry and beadlily.

You know you're close to the river when you see a wide open expanse ahead, the Dark River valley. It varies in width and openness. Here it's about 90 yards across from high point to high point. The point you are on is approximately 40 feet above the river itself. The

97

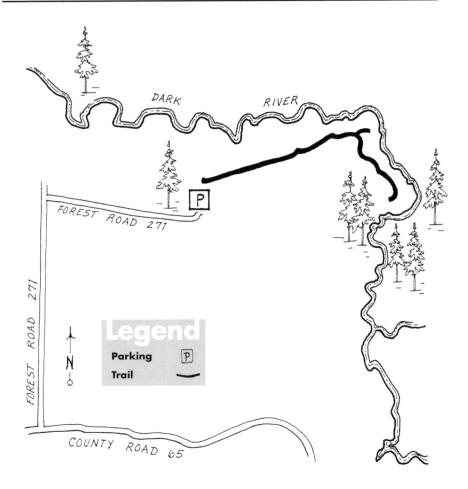

trail veers right near the river and then climbs another 20 feet. Note the stumps along the trail, evidence of aspen felled by beavers for building material and food.

You'll reach an area along the bank that has eroded, with trees, brush, and dirt having slipped off the hillside into the river. This natural catastrophe has provided a clear view of a bend in the river directly below. Just on the left, in the river, is a beaver dam. Willow and alder crowd the river, challenging its flow all the while the water nourishes them.

The trail is tricky here for about 10 yards, becoming a little footpath in the newly exposed dirt (or slippery mud) on the side of the eroded hill. A slip here will land you 30 feet below in the alder and river muck.

You'll eventually wind down the path to the river, passing through some thick alder on the way. As you approach the river, listen for the slap of a beaver's tail as it warns its companions of your approach. There's another beaver dam on the left, seemingly abandoned, and a newer one to the right. A hawthorn tree, looking like a shrub, grows on the riverbank, on the left of the trail as you face the river. Wild roses struggle for space between alder and hazel along here too.

When you turn back from the river, retrace your path about 20 feet and bear left on the trail, which will take you back up along the higher riverbank. There are several good views of the river valley along this section, including the tops of a dense thicket of alder. Be glad you're not trudging through that.

You'll then pass a grove of red pine; these have been naturally seeded, as shown by their variation in age and size. The trail then drops back down near the river again, winding through a lovely white spruce, aspen, and jack pine woods. Soon you'll see a large expanse of red pine. These were planted in the 1930s by the Civilian Conservation Corps. Even though they are about 60 years old, they are not very large; trees grow slowly here. At this point, the path gradually slants away from the river. It also widens and shows evidence of use by wheeled vehicles. You can turn around anytime and head back the way you came in.

Sturgeon River Trail
Superior National Forest

Distance: 6 miles, one way

Time: 2.5 to 3 hours

Path: The walking is easy on the first half of this hike. Then things get tougher, as the trail winds through areas of bunchgrass and unmowed forest plants. The trail marking is also spotty. There are a few small cross-country-ski signs, easy to miss in the summer woods. The clear-cut area is particularly confounding, all the more because you are not near enough to the river to use it as a guide. So make sure to bring a compass.

Directions: From Chisholm, take Highway 73 north for 12 miles to County Highway 65. Turn left (west) on 65 and go 1.3 miles to the parking area on the right. Since this walk is 6 miles one way, you may want to leave a car or bike where the hike ends, 2.3 miles farther north on Highway 73, where the road crosses the Sturgeon River.

Contact: Superior National Forest, Laurentian Ranger District, 318 Forestry Road, Aurora, MN 55705; (218)229-3371.

Highlights: The shelter overlooking the river, near the middle of this hike provides a wonderful place to rest and relax amid pines near a lovely river. The river meanders near the end of the hike, and there are plenty of opportunities to watch the wildlife.

Finding the trail at the beginning of this hike can be tricky. Climb the steep but short hill at the northwest corner of the parking area, where there is a trail sign. Once you're atop the hill and entering the wooded area, the trail curves gently left through a small clearing. Watch for a trail sign where you reenter the woods from the clearing. If you don't see the sign, don't enter the woods; go back to the clearing and look again for the sign.

The trail skirts a large clear-cut on the right for several hundred yards, then enters a dense pine woods. The steep slope on your left leads eventually to the Sturgeon River. You won't see the river for some time, but there are occasional views of its broad pine-graced valley.

The trail makes a series of short, 15-foot drops, then regains the lost altitude while it snakes through various types of woodlands. Several times it flirts with clear-cut areas where raspberry, various ferns, and fireweed grow rampant. At one point you'll walk through

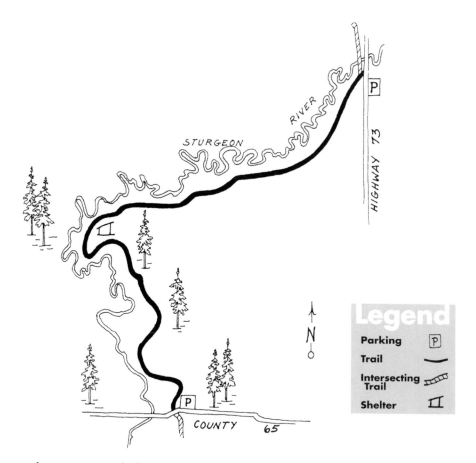

STURGEON RIVER

HIGHWAY 73

N

COUNTY 65

Legend

Parking	P
Trail	—
Intersecting Trail	
Shelter	

an almost pure stand of red pine, with a few jack pine mixed in. The stand is likely the result of a fire many years ago, since red and jack pine seed germinate best on mineral soil and in full light.

The forest floor here is a thick carpet of needles, offering enjoyable walking. Yet there is something odd about the trail surface. Into it have been gouged numerous holes the size of baseballs and even basketballs; these depressions occur along the entire remaining trail. While they are not a problem here amid the clean and uncluttered pine needle surface, they become treacherous farther on when they are partially covered by grasses and leaves. So beware.

When you reach an area where the trail is covered with bunchgrass and you begin seeing alder, you are near a clear-cut that makes for much more difficult hiking and gives a preview of the type of trail surface you'll encounter later on. Once the trail exits the clear-cut, it begins a slow decent to nearer the river. Then, amid some pleasantly large pine, you'll see the river for the first time on the left, and a shelter with a bench on your right. Plop down and rest a bit—you're almost halfway through the journey. Or you can wander off the trail a bit to the left and check out the river. The bank is steep, so be careful; and don't walk where severe erosion has occurred.

After your respite, continue on down the trail. Following a brief stint in some pines, you'll climb to another clear-cut area, then hike amid some small, widely scattered popple and spruce. The trail is mostly grass here, but the footing has become less sure because the ground is full of the same kinds of large holes you encountered earlier. Soon you'll see a vast sea of small red pine planted in the 1980s. The trail stays near the river for a while, providing some nice views of the water. Then the path turns right, away from the river, and enters the red pine plantation. The openness of it is striking. Note the copse of aspen that stand starkly tall and limbless to 60 feet in height. Deer tracks mark the sandy trail.

As you traverse this open area, look for an odd-looking structure supported by stilts. It's undoubtedly someone's deer hunting stand, but it's so elaborate it could be a cabin. Watch for it several hundred yards away on the right side of the trail, not long before it enters a grove of black ash trees. When you exit the black ash, it's important that you begin looking carefully for a little blue arrow-shaped trail marker on a post that points you down a trail that cuts left. Follow this path, off the trail you have been on and are likely to follow if you miss the arrow. If you overlooked this junction and are on the wrong trail, don't panic. Use your compass and head straight east; Highway 73 is just over a half mile away.

The trail you should be on hugs the river again, but now lower and closer to it. The path dips down into and crosses several small ravines, which will be wet and muddy in the spring and in rainy weather. Some of the crossings have plank bridges. Along here are good places for taking a side trip to the river, where you'll see lots of silver maples, fast-growing, water-loving trees with silvery green leaves.

There is plenty of evidence of beaver activity along the trail here and more of those mysterious holes in the ground. Perhaps fox have dug the holes, or woodchucks.

Soon you'll be able to hear highway sounds. After crossing a bridge made from an old Forest Service sign (the word *Eveleth* is still readable), you'll climb up onto the roadway near the Highway 73 bridge over the Sturgeon River. This is the end of the trail.

Shingobee Recreation Area Trail
Chippewa National Forest

Distance: 3 miles

Time: 1 hour

Path: A mowed-grass surface, well marked with map boards at most intersections. The rolling and hilly terrain is moderately difficult.

Directions: From the intersection of Highways 200 and 34 in Walker, take Highway 34 south for 6 miles. Look for the Shingobee Recreation Area sign on the left.

Contact: Chippewa National Forest, Walker District, 201 Minnesota Ave. East, Walker, MN 56484; (218)547-1044.

Highlights: The is a hilly hike, with some nice vistas of distant tree lines and one lovely little lake. Part of the walk is on the famous North Country Trail.

Start this trek from the circular parking area just off the highway. Walk south into a clearing, which is actually a large, curved, treeless hillside that slopes away from the parking area. From here you can see several distant ridge tops and picture what an impressive toboggan hill it must be in the winter. This entire recreation area was developed back in the 1930s as a winter sports complex, and the hill in front of you was once a downhill-ski slope.

Make a left turn at the top of the hill and follow the mowed path into the woods. The trail begins to drop almost immediately. The slope is steep, both down and then up. If you're hiking in the mid-morning on a sunny day, the bottoms of the ravines will be noticeably cooler than the tops.

After traversing several such dips, you'll reach the first intersection, where you'll bear left. You'll first encounter some large jack pine, then hike through a stand of small, pole-sized aspen. Under the aspen along the trail's edge, there are hundreds of plants called cohosh, a common understory wildflower that rarely is seen growing as thickly as it is here. Also interspersed alongside the trail are occasional blackberry plants, which produce giant thumb-sized berries in August. On

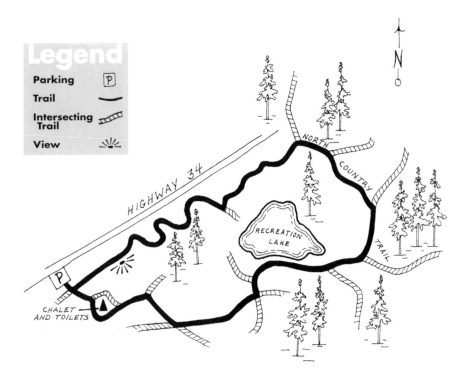

another downhill pitch, you'll see the trail edge draped with bracken fern.

The next junction is marked by a large signboard that describes the North Country Trail, which runs 3,200 miles from Crown Point, New York, to Lake Sakakawea, North Dakota. The next half mile of this walk is on part of the 68 miles of the trail that crosses the Chippewa National Forest.

The trail cuts through a plantation of 10- to 15-year-old red pine, then dips down into a low area, where white spruce and balsam fir grow. According to the Forest Service, *shingobee* is an Ojibwa word for cedar, spruce, and balsam trees. You won't see Shingobee's third namesake tree, cedar, here anymore because high deer populations prevent new stands from becoming established.

Bearing to the right at the next two intersections, you'll continue on the North Country Trail back onto higher ground, through some tall pine and along one of the few flat stretches of this hike. Watch for a couple of enormous red pine, nearly 3 feet in diameter, along the trail here.

At the next junction, bear right again. You'll leave the North Country Trail here and hike down a long downhill stretch to where you can see Recreation Lake on the right. The trail then climbs up onto a ridge that provides several nice vistas of the lake through some middle-aged red pine.

With the lake receding behind you as you continue your journey, turn left at the next junction and then, only about 50 feet farther, right at the next. Now you'll be on an old logging road that has been used in the past as an access to the area you've already hiked. There are lots of gopher mounds (but few holes) all along this road.

By turning right at the next junction you'll find yourself in a meadow that is abundant with wildflowers: blazing star, dotted mint, goldenrod, sunflower, aster, black-eyed Susan, and daisies, to name a few. Straight ahead the toboggan hill will come into view. Walk around its base to the left, past the chalet, which is only open in the winter, and back into the woods near the toilets. After a steep climb back up the hill and then a left turn at the top, you're back at the parking area.

Pondview Interpretive Trail
Sibley State Park

Distance: 1 mile

Time: 1 hour

Path: Dirt and mowed grass. The path is uneven, especially around the pond area. There are moderate hills, steep but not long. Trail marking is excellent.

Directions: From the junction of Highway 71 and County Highway 48 approximately 15 miles north of Willmar, take County 48 west for less than a mile into the park.

Contact: Sibley State Park, 800 Sibley Park Road N.E., New London, MN 56273; (320)354-2055.

Highlights: The pond provides an excellent niche for diverse wildlife and flora. Besides an incredible number of birds, there are several types of frogs, turtles, and even salamanders. Small mammals enjoy the area too, and you may see muskrats, minks, rabbits, and gophers.

I f you're wondering how Sibley State Park got its name, it was named for Harry Hastings Sibley, the state's first governor, who did a lot of hunting in the area.

Start your hike from the southeast corner of the interpretive center parking lot, where a wooden sign identifies the trail. Hike up a small hill and you'll soon encounter a signboard and a fork in the trail. Take the right fork and enter a lovely bur oak woods. Follow the trail as it winds gently downhill toward another signboard, this one identifying the trail and describing its features.

Before you lies the pond, about seven acres in size and bordered by cattails and other herbaceous wetland plants. Trees, mostly bur oak, are visible along the ridges above the pond. Depending on the time of year, you'll see lots of birds: Canada geese, mallards, and blue-wing teal frequent the pond; and bluebirds, tanager, red-winged blackbirds, and many other varieties like the surrounding wetlands and uplands.

Bear right from the sign. You'll see many plants here that are typical of the area. In late summer and fall, there are asters and goldenrods. Milkweeds also abound, even the lovely yellow-gold butterfly weed. In early summer, great lobelia and bladderwort also grace the landscape here.

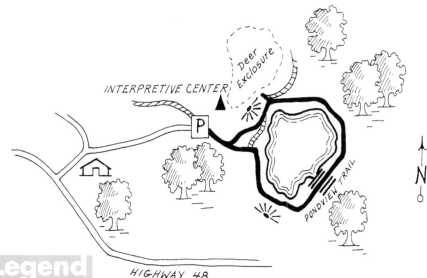

INTERPRETIVE CENTER

Deer Exclosure

P

PONDVIEW TRAIL

N

HIGHWAY 48

Parking   P

Trail

Intersecting Trail

Bridge

View

One of the signboards along the trail tells about the Prairie Pothole Region. This is a 300,000-square-mile area stretching from the Canadian province of Alberta on the north and west, through southern Saskatchewan and Manitoba, then down through parts of North and South Dakota, Minnesota, and finally Iowa. It is one of the richest wetlands in the world, despite the fact that over 50 percent of it has been taken over by roads, agriculture, and buildings.

The trail then traces the edge of the pond and climbs a little hill, where a bench has been thoughtfully placed for hikers who want to sit a while and watch the water. Next, the trail dips down to a bridge that crosses a narrow spot in the pond. As you cross, look below into the water near the posts supporting the bridge. There you'll see thousands of snail shells of several kinds—escargot for pond predators!

Walk up onto the little ridge along the east end of the pond. Here you'll find more wildflowers and perhaps glimpse one of the park's many animals: a buck fleeing from your intrusion, a racoon leaving his breakfast along the pond's edge, or a mink slinking into the high grass.

As you walk, look up ahead. You can see several very large trees, their silvery leaves contrasting with the oaks along the ridge in front of you. These are nonnative poplar that were planted here by settlers around 1900. As you walk to the edge of the woods near the trees, you can also see a large flowering crab planted by the settlers. A little wooden sign marks their homestead. There is not much left of the original dwelling: a fieldstone wall, likely the foundation, and some concrete slabs in front of the foundation, perhaps a front porch. Stand on what is left of the porch and look toward the pond, as the former occupants surely did. The view is framed by a big old juniper on the left and several large bur oak on the right. What a wonderful place to start and end the day.

As you continue the walk, you'll reach an intersection. You'll eventually go left, but first you'll take a short detour to the right, up a hill and past the sign that reads "Deer Exclosure." The mowed trail takes you to a 10-foot-high fence that encloses an area of about a thousand square feet. The purpose of the fencing is to keep out deer so that park personnel and visitors can observe and study a nonbrowsed area. This one has something truly amazing growing inside it: 10 amur maple, in a perfectly straight row, have sprouted and grown 15 feet. Since this plant is native to northern Siberia, one can only guess how it managed to grow in an area meant for observing native vegetation and the area's reaction to being free of deer browse.

Following the mowed trail as it loops down off the hill will afford you a nice view of another pond and the interpretive center on its far shore. You'll then complete the loop, ending up back near the homestead at the previous junction. Head straight (this would have been a left as you exited the homestead area) and climb another hill to a bench, where there is another wonderful view of both ponds. After bearing to the right at the junction here, you'll get one more glimpse of the interpretive center and its pond, then reach the little spur trail from the parking area where you began this pleasant stroll. Make a right turn and you'll see your vehicle as you top the small hill.

Lawrence Headquarters Loop
Minnesota Valley State Recreation Area

Distance: 1.5 miles

Time: 1 hour

Path: The trail width varies from about 6 to more than 8 feet. The surface is mowed grass, except in heavily shaded areas where there is more mud than grass. The path is well marked, and staying on it is easy. There are a few modest hills, but the route is essentially flat.

Directions: From the intersection of Highways 25 and 169 in Belle Plaine, take Highway 169 northeast approximately 2 miles to County Road 57. Go left on 57 just over 2 miles to the Lawrence headquarters building on the right and park in the lot.

Contact: Minnesota Valley State Recreation Area, 19825 Park Boulevard, Jordan, MN 55352; (612) 492-6400.

Highlights: This is an easy and quick stroll through a diverse landscape of plants. There are wetland plants along the river and upland types on the rest of the hike, including some big, old bur oak.

From the headquarters parking lot, walk back out to the county road, then turn left and go about a quarter mile to where the trail intersects the road. Turn right onto the trail and head into the woods, where you'll be greeted by some lovely old basswood, white ash, and red and white oak. This section is the most heavily wooded part of the hike. The trail pitches gradually downhill for the next eighth of a mile and then reaches a map board and junction, where you'll turn right. Check out the stand of smaller trees behind the map board. These are mulberry, a fast-growing and, some would say, weedy tree, which produces large amounts of fruit that look like raspberries but have an insipid flavor. Birds love the berries, however, so it's a great wildlife tree.

After passing several massive white oak trees, you'll reach a clearing whose edge is marked by staghorn sumac, which blaze brilliant red-orange in the fall. Once in the clearing, look left and you'll see a backwater of the Minnesota River, perhaps an old channel. It's a prime

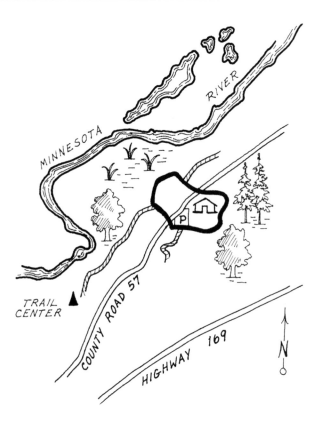

Legend

Parking [P]

Trail —

Intersecting Trail

Park Office

Marsh

MINNESOTA RIVER

TRAIL CENTER ▲

COUNTY ROAD 57

HIGHWAY 169

N

habitat for ducks. Listen for them. And look for bald eagles, who sometimes dine on the ducks.

As you progress farther into the clearing, note the small trees that dot it. Most of these are green ash and box elder, both tough, fast-growing trees that grow in a wide range of environments. Look back toward the water on your left. Near the east end of the wet area are several muskrat houses. Often called marsh rats, these creatures build moundlike dwellings out of cattails and mud, then spend the winter in them.

When the trail curves right, cast your gaze left at a stand of small box elder in the foreground and at a wetland beyond. If you look hard you'll see a well-traveled deer trail that disappears into the box elder. And you'll easily spot the trail in the fall, when it gets heavy traffic from the animals.

After the curve you'll come to a junction. You should continue straight, up a slight grade toward County Road 57. You'll see some trees on your left and then a shallow gully, which deepens as you get closer to the road. Note the piles of rocks in the gully. When the field on your right was farmed many years ago, thousands of rocks were hauled out of it and dumped there.

Continue across the county road. About 10 yards beyond it, you'll see a mowed path to the right, then an old headstone. The inscription on it is almost impossible to read. The date 1860 is legible, but you can't tell if this is the date of the deceased's birth or death. It seems certain that this is the gravesite of an early settler, perhaps the person who labored moving the many stones you saw back in the gully.

As you continue your walk, you'll begin seeing red cedar trees: an evergreen more properly called juniper. The trees are native but have become unwelcome invaders of many prairies in the region. Also many large bur oak populate this section of trail. Soon you'll begin seeing a barbed-wire fence on the left that marks the recreation area's south boundary. Stay along the fence until the trail makes a right turn. After the turn, you'll notice a difference in the vegetation along the trail. The brush is thicker, and there are more shrubs such as hazelnut, red and gray dogwood, and shrubby willows.

The trail then crosses an almost imperceptible gully on a 10-foot-long span of planks and passes a copse of small very white-barked aspen on the right. You'll notice a path on the left that has been hacked through the brush. About 30 feet down it a small wooden structure sits on a metal post. It looks like a large birdhouse, perhaps for wood ducks, since it borders an open area that is probably wet in the spring.

Go back to the main trail, bear left, and soon you'll see some park buildings on the right. This is the headquarters and parking lot area. Continue down the trail and, after passing through more thick brush that is made even denser by intertwining grapevines, you'll reach a junction and signboard. Go right and you'll be back in the thick woods that greeted you when you started the walk. Walk only a few hundred feet back to the road, go right, and return to the parking area where you left your vehicle.

Vistas, Views, and Overlooks

Oberg Mountain Loop
Superior National Forest

Distance: 2 miles

Time: 1 to 2 hours

Path: Consists of crushed rock for the first few hundred feet but soon becomes rocky and root infested. The climb is gradual but continual for the first .5 mile or so. Once on top of the mountain, the path circles around on granite outcrops and through mountain-top woods. It's easy to follow but has precipitous edges at the overlooks.

Directions: From Tofte, take Highway 61 northeast for 5 miles to Forest Road 336 (Onion River Road). Go left on 336 about 2 miles. The parking area is on the left and the trailhead on the right.

Contact: Forest Supervisor, Superior National Forest, P.O. Box 338, Duluth, MN 55801; (218)626-4300; or Tofte Ranger District, Tofte, MN 55615; (218)663-7280.

Highlights: This trail is unusual in that it loops around the top of Oberg Mountain, with nine scenic overlooks for wonderful views of inland hills and Lake Superior's shoreline. Wisconsin's Bayfield Peninsula and some of the Apostle Islands are also visible on a clear day.

For the first quarter mile of the hike, the trail climbs slowly upward, through a stand of large cedar, birch, and spruce, then loops through a sugar maple woods. When the trail switches back right and continues its ascent, look right. Off in the distance, over the trail you just climbed, you can see the parking area below far below!

Just 20 minutes or so after leaving the parking area, you'll join the loop that circles the mountain top and arrive at the first of nine overlooks. This one looks back to the parking lot and to a hill beyond. The next, only about 100 feet farther down the trail, provides a view of several hills, one with a flat, buttelike top. To the left, Lake Superior stretches toward the horizon.

After entering and exiting a lovely and dark maple woods, which occupies a swale on the mountaintop, you'll see a rough-hewn wood bench sitting atop a large granite slab at the next vista point. The view is due south, right at the big lake. On a clear day you can see

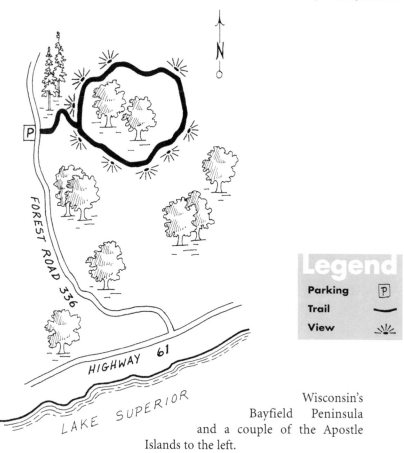

Legend

Parking	P
Trail	—
View	☆

Wisconsin's Bayfield Peninsula and a couple of the Apostle Islands to the left.

Reenter the maple woods, which here includes some ash, and hike to the next overlook. A rustic picnic table greets you, carved from logs with a chain saw. The view is to the southeast squarely at the Apostle Islands. A nearby bluff top overlooks the north shore as you direct your gaze up the line where water meets land. The same bluff is visible from the next vista, where you also can view more of the interior highlands to the left. A sixth overlook points you north, at the highland hills, but the northerly trending shoreline is still visible off to the far right. This is an outstanding view in the fall, when the highland maples and oaks are in color.

At the next overlook, our seventh, a wood rail fence guards the edge of the granite slab. A glance below shows why. A good 200-foot sheer drop is all there is, then a rough slope full of talus. An inland lake is visible to the left. You're on the northwest side of the mountain now, and the trees near the edge are small, stunted, and often blown over.

The next-to-last overlook is just a short hike away. It looks almost due west, directly at the small lake. Note the bog north of the lake and the conifers that grow on the bog edge. From this angle, the different ecological niches look very distinct. Spruce and fir forest blend into a tamarack and cedar bog, which gives way to a low bog and then the lake. As the trail leads away from this overlook and into a lower protected area, note how the trees are larger than those near the cliff edge, with more maple in the mix. You'll then loop back up and out to the next, and last, overlook, which has two ledges in a stepping-stone formation. The view from either step is pleasing. The little lake is still directly below, and the large area of wetland and bog stretch out to the right of the lake. An extensive black spruce bog surrounds the entire area. Look hard for moose; they inhabit areas like this.

As you walk away from this view back into the mountaintop woods, notice that a 100-yard section of trail is surrounded by young trees only, the older ones having been blown down 25 or 30 years ago. Big spruce mark the edge of the once-devastated area. It's only a couple of hundred yards until you reach the trail junction, where a right turn and a walk on the trail that brought you up the mountain will now take you back to the parking area.

Observation Tower Walk
Mille Lacs Kathio State Park

Distance: .5 mile, round trip

Time: 30 minutes

Path: After an easy walk over mowed grass on a moderate ascent to the tower, the climb up the wooden steps of the steel frame tower isn't for the fainthearted.

Directions: From the intersection of Highway 169 and County Highway 26 on the southwest shore of Mille Lacs, take 26 for 1 mile south to the park entrance. Then take the park road to the Ogechie Lake campground and park your vehicle in the area provided.

Contact: Mille Lacs Kathio State Park, 15066 Kathio State Park Road, Onamia, MN 56359; (320)532-3523.

Highlights: This walk affords you a great view from an old fire tower of Mille Lacs, the second largest lake fully within the boundaries of Minnesota, and a look at the smallest wildlife refuge in the nation.

Start your walk from the parking area near the trail center, then hike up the road until you reach a wide road-wide trail that goes right. This trail winds through forest for about a quarter mile, ascending the entire way until it reaches the fire tower. After climbing more than 100 wooden steps to its top, you'll see the lake stretching south and east. The view is impressive. When standing on shore, you can't see the other side of the lake, but from this observation point the entire 207 square miles of water are visible. The distance to the farthest shore in sight is about 22 miles.

Looking just about due north, you'll see Rainbow Island off a point of land. As you to the left, you'll make out a ribbon of water, or at least a break in the forest canopy, which is first Ogechie Lake. It becomes the Rum River as you gaze farther south. Shakopee Lake is visible to the southwest.

The tower sits atop a glacial moraine, a pile of rocks and dirt that marks the farthest extent of the glacier. The Rum River is the only outlet for Mille Lacs. The lake exists because 10,000 years ago the glacier carved out its basin and then deposited much of the debris right below you, blocking the flow of water to the south.

Another piece of glacial debris lies out in the lake. If you look toward the northeast, you'll barely be able to make out Spirit Island, a quarter-acre agglomeration of rocks. It and its slightly larger sister island, Hennepin, comprise the Mille Lacs National Wildlife Refuge, the smallest such refuge in the country. The refuge protects critical nesting areas for the common tern, a bird that, as it turns out, is decidedly uncommon. About a quarter of Minnesota's nesting pair population of 400 terns make nests in May on these two islands.

Sunrise and sunset viewed from the tower can be awe inspiring. If you can time your climb accordingly, you'll be rewarded.

When you're ready, retrace your steps to the parking area. You're finished with this walk.

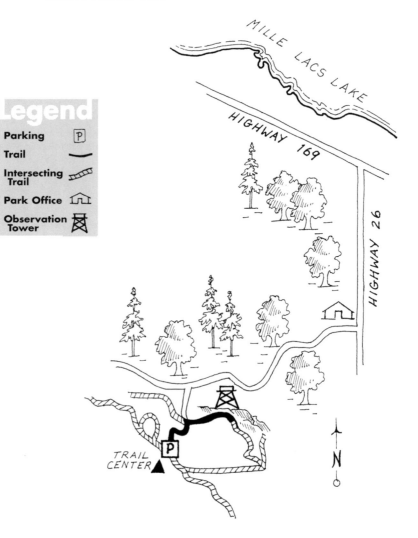

Mount Tom Overlook
Sibley State Park

Distance: .25 mile, not including the climb up the tower

Time: 30 minutes; it could be much longer if you decide the view is as wonderful as most folks consider it to be.

Path: Asphalt.

Directions: From the junction of Highway 71 and County Highway 48 approximately 15 miles north of Willmar, take County 48 west for less than a mile into the park.

Contact: Sibley State Park, 800 Sibley Park Road N.E., New London, MN 56273; (320)354-2055.

Highlights: This walk is short but very sweet. The view from the observation tower is stunning. It's the highest point for about 50 miles and the architecture of the tower alone is worth the trip.

Start at the east side of the Mount Tom parking area. The asphalt trail is narrow, so it is not too roadlike. The forest is almost all bur oak, of all sizes. There is one lone hackberry alongside the trail on the left, about 20 feet from the parking lot.

At the end of October or the beginning of November, all the oaks have dropped their leaves and the ground is thick with them. Yet you'll often see them pushed into little piles, with bare ground visible here and there. Three different culprits are the possible cause of this leaf pushing. All are searching for acorns. Deer paw at the leaves to uncover the tasty morsels. And everyone has seen gray squirrels mess around in leaves looking for food. What's the third possibility? Turkeys love it here, and they can scratch up a leaf storm, rendering huge areas of the forest floor look a leafy mess.

As you follow the gentle curve of the hill, climbing all the way, you'll notice the tower above you and off to the right. From a distance it looks like a Japanese pagoda. As you continue hiking upward, you will see sumac covering the hillside between you and the tower. They make an impressive display in the fall, red and orange leaves blazing in the September sun. On your left the ground falls away, into a ravine of sorts. And bur oak wrap their ample limbs around the hillside as it slopes downward.

You'll then reach the bottom of some steps, which lead up to the tower. There are three sets of steps, arranged in groups of four. Each set has a small landing made of aggregate-faced concrete paving blocks. Stand at the bottom of the steps and gaze upward at the tower. From this vantage point, it retains its pagoda-like features, especially the shape of the roof. But it's the structure's pedestal of lovely granite blocks that you'll find most intriguing. They vary in size and shape: some are slabs measuring 12 by 30 by 5 inches, and others are blocks 18 by 18 by 24 inches. The pedestal is uniquely shaped: 4 trapezoids set on their long parallel sides. At each edge, where the trapezoids meet, is a set of blocks, flowing downward and forming a knee near the base. Signboards sit on each knee.

On top of each knee are signboards with information about Mount Tom. On one there are old pictures of the summit and a bit of history about the place. Surprisingly, no one knows why this hill is named Tom. Another signboard deals with geology. The mount and the surrounding topography are part of the Alexandria Moraine complex, a landform that stretches from Detroit Lakes in the north to Willmar in the south. The complex varies from 7 to 15 miles in width. It is the result of the area's last glacier, known as the Wisconsin, but it was also shaped by over two million years of previous glacial activity. A few facts that you won't learn on the summit are that it's 1,375 feet above sea level and is the highest point for about 50 miles. Hence the great view.

And, of course, partaking of the view involves climbing up the tower. Unlike many towers in state parks, this one should inspire confidence in everyone but the most die-hard acrophobes. The steps are substantial and they lead you up to what is really the second floor of the tower. And at the top you'll find informative and easy-to-use panoramic pictures of the surrounding area, with lakes and towns marked so you can identify what you are looking at.

It's not often that the architecture of an observation tower rivals the view, but this one does. Both are great. Then retrace your steps to return to the parking lot.

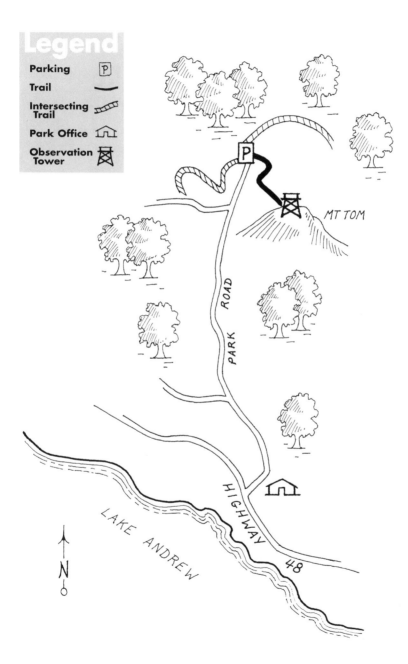

Legend

Parking   P

Trail

Intersecting Trail

Park Office

Observation Tower

MT TOM

PARK ROAD

HIGHWAY 48

LAKE ANDREW

N

37

Seven Overlooks Hike
Great River Bluffs State Park

Distance: 8 miles if shuttled back from the campground to the parking area; 10 miles if you hike back by the shortest route

Time: 3 to 4 hours

Path: Various surfaces but mostly mowed grass; the path through the woods consists of dirt and can be muddy. This is an easy hike of significant distance.

Directions: From the intersection of I-90 and Highway 61 in Dakota, take I-90 4 miles west to exit 266 at County Highway 12. Exit right onto Highway 12, then take an immediate right on County Highway 3. Follow Highway 3 approximately 1 mile to the park entrance on the right.

Contact: Great River Bluffs State Park, Route 4, Winona, MN 55987; (507)643-6849.

Highlights: Lots of overlooks for views up, down, and across the mighty Mississippi. You can also see several goat prairies, unique ecological niches where only tough plants survive.

The ridge-top ride into the park hints at what lies ahead on this hike. The park road follows a spine of 1,200-foot-high land that reaches to within about a quarter mile of the Mississippi. Start hiking from the parking area on the left, a third of a mile past the information booth at the park entrance. The mowed path is inviting, with rows of plantation white pine on your right and an old field to the left. A sign tells about Henslow's sparrow, rare in Minnesota but found to nest in this field. Soon the path enters the plantation and becomes a canopied corridor paved with pine needles.

Take a left at the next map board. The trail loops out of the pines and into another plantation, this one composed of green ash. The loop continues, past a couple of apple trees on the left and a lovely 20-foot-tall nannyberry (*Viburnum lentago*).

After a short climb, you'll arrive at a vista point, with a bench on the left and a trail junction to the right, that provides a spectacular view of the Mississippi and the bluffs on the Wisconsin side. There's also a nice view of a goat prairie on the side of the nearest bluff. Goat prairies are so called because their steepness precludes all creatures but surefooted goats from spending much time on them. The terrain's lack of woody vegetation results from its harsh environment. The 40- to 50-degree slope not only collects a lot of sun and therefore heat, both summer and winter, but also sheds water, a characteristic that makes it all the more arid. Only grasses and other tough prairie vegetation can tolerate these sites.

Go left when you've ready to move on, because there are several more wonderful views ahead. Soon you'll see a large signboard that tells about the geology of the area. Some 500 million years ago a vast part of the continent, including the area that is now Minnesota and Wisconsin, was under an ocean. (While 500 million years is nearly incomprehensible, this may help: 500 million years is to one year, as one year is to less than half a second.) The bluff you are standing on, the spine of land the park road occupies, and indeed all such higher, flatter areas were formed when sediment was deposited on the bottom of this ocean. When the great glacier melted 10,000 years ago, torrents of water flowed from it toward the Mississippi, eroding the countryside and creating the rugged coulee country we see today.

A sign soon notes your passage into the King's Bluff State Natural Area. The path narrows and winds gracefully through the forested bluff top. Shagbark hickory grows here, near the limit of its range. Poison ivy flourishes also, as evidenced by the one- and two-inch-thick vines snaking 30 feet up numerous tree trunks.

As the forest thins out, you'll approach another scenic view and the end of this trail. The first view is to the north and west, away from the river. Below is a pastoral setting rivaling any Norman Rockwell painting. After the path traces its final few yards through and next to a restored prairie, you'll get a glimpse of the river. Depending on the weather and the sun's angle, the water may be a dull gray, a bright silver, or any one of 50 shades of blue. Beyond the river channel is a large wetland, and then the Wisconsin bluffs. The wetland and a break in the bluffs outline the mouth of the Black River. Directly below, almost invisible but clearly audible, are Highways 14 and 61 and a set of railroad tracks. The nearest bluff, with a goat prairie top, is Queens Bluff, also the site of a state natural area.

When you're ready, retrace your path back to the first view of the Mississippi. Take the left trail, which runs along the edge of the slope. There are several trails that go right; but if you keep left, you'll walk around the semicircle that forms the head of the valley between King's and Queen's Bluffs. Downhill will always be on your left. That way also lies an enormous stand of staghorn sumac, with some plants over 30 feet high and thicker than a marathon runner's calf.

The trail then makes a T-shaped junction. A left turn takes you a couple of hundred yards toward Queen's Bluff but provides no view, ending amid poison ivy and dense woods. The natural area at Queen's

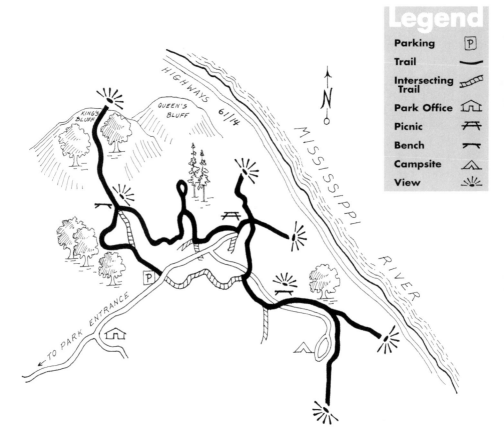

Bluff is closed because it's a sanctuary for several rare plants. Turn right and trek through a pine plantation for about 200 yards to a signboard, where you'll bear left. The trail skirts a small pond marked by numerous deer trails leading toward it. (Despite its presence here, water is a bit hard to find in the area close to the top of the ridge.)

At the next signboard, turn right and you'll reach the park road in less than 100 yards. Bear left and walk the road into a picnic area. Continue in the same direction until you come to a sign that says "Hiking Trail." About 50 feet farther lie another signboard and trail junction. Turn left and hug the top of a steep slope until you reach a wood-railed overlook. The panorama is similar to the one at King's Bluff, except that Queen's Bluff isn't in the way. The drop from the overlook is impressive. It's only a quarter mile to the river, plus about 500 vertical feet.

Return to the signboard and take a left at the trail junction 10 feet beyond. It's about 180 yards to the next scenic view, the first of the vantage points to face in a southerly direction. Out of sight farther down river, the Dresbach Lock and Dam blocks the river, and you can begin seeing a widening here. This is the northern beginning of Lake Onalaska.

Hike back to the main trail and make a hard left down a long, steep hill. This is a ski trail in winter, and skiers certainly encounter a challenge with this downhill. In fact, there's a big banged-up old white oak at the bottom of the hill, near the edge of the trail. One wonders if the missing bark is the result of trail-grooming machines or skiers.

You'll regain the altitude you lost descending the ski hill, then cross the park road once again. Make a left at the next signboard. The trail parallels the park road, dipping down into a ravine, which can be muddy in the spring or after a major rainfall. You'll then reach yet another signboard (this park is well marked!), where you'll turn left and head back across the road one more time. On the other side, the trail takes you through some small maple trees and a couple of wonderfully gnarly old bur and white oaks. When you reach a bench near the road, sit a while and enjoy the overlook, which opens out onto the goat prairie below the last overlook you were on. From here the trail again parallels the road, passing some venerable oaks any squirrel would be proud to call home.

The trail then splits into two, and another signboard greets you near the circle drive into the campground. Follow the trail left, along the 1,200-foot-high spine of land that takes you to an overlook, this one facing the south and the Mississippi.

When you're ready, retrace your steps back to the signboard near the campground, then continue down the path that roughly parallels the circle drive for about 75 feet until you reach another signboard and trail junction. Turn left here and hike through some small trees and large shrubs as you loop around the campground and out another spine of land to the last overlook. When you reach it, several bluffs will block your view of the river, but you can look down at a coulee, the home of a Dakota Creek tributary. To the south, the interstate winds its way up and down the bluffs. Below and to the right, an oddly symmetrical plantation of green ash or black walnut fills the valley floor.

Retrace your steps back to the campground. If you've left a vehicle there, your hike is over. If you need to retrieve it from the parking lot, you can get there via two routes: follow the park road back to it or reenter the winding hiking trail to the left where it crosses the park road, about a half mile from the campground. One caution: the trail is intersected by several mowed cross-country-ski trails and can be confusing. If you're tired from all the climbing and gazing, it might be wise to stick to the park road.

Riverview Trail
John Latsch State Park

Distance: .5 mile, round trip

Time: How quickly can you climb 598 steps? The view is impressive, so count on at least 30 minutes.

Path: The walk is on mowed grass through the picnic area to the first set of steps, with a couple of very short segments on bedrock and dirt. The rest is on wooden steps and platforms.

Directions: From the village of Minneiska (19 miles south of Wabasha), go south on Highway 61 approximately 2 miles. The park entrance is on the right and not well identified, so be ready to turn.

Contact: Whitewater State Park, Route 1, Box 256, Altura, MN 55910; (507)932-3007. (John Latsch State Park is small and in the process of being developed. It doesn't have an information station or park headquarters.)

Highlights: Although the trail is short, it takes you to one of the best Mississippi River views on the Minnesota side. Plus, the area is steeped in cultural and natural history. The park has been has been undergoing a recent transition from wayside park to full-fledged state park, a move that visitors will applaud.

The bluff whose top the Riverview Trail labors toward is called Mount Charity. Old navigation charts used by river pilots in the 1800s identified the two sister bluffs south of Mount Charity as Mount Hope and Mount Faith. There used to be a steamboat landing and small town at the base of these bluffs, but they were flooded by the pool above Lock and Dam No. 5.

Let's begin hiking. The sign for the Riverview Trail is in the southwest corner of the little picnic area just beyond the first parking area. As you enter the trail, look to the left and you'll see a gigantic white oak, about 3 feet in diameter. Then take a deep breath and start climbing the path. There are two benches on the right. A sign inscribed "Ray Silver 1918–1979" and "Marjorie McComb Silver 1930–" identifies two park benefactors. Mrs. Silver still climbs to the top of the bluff and loves the view. Feel humbled (and inspired) and continue climbing.

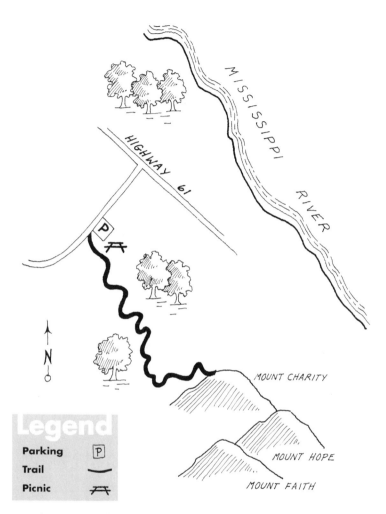

When you reach the first set of steps with a railing, look off to the left, and if the foliage isn't too thick you can begin to see swatches of blue river below you. The second set of railings means you've reached the "ladder section." The rise on these steps is a couple of inches higher than that on the rest of the stairs, making this section of the climb more ladderlike. Bare rock outcrops are a clue that you're getting closer to the top. So are the treetops that you can actually reach out and touch. Mostly white birch at this point, they are small and weathered, indicative of a tough life here, growing on thin soil and buffeted by fierce winds.

Soon you'll come to a break in the steps. At the edge of the bluff, you can gaze north and east across the river. Silos from Wisconsin farms poke their round heads over the distant rim of the Mississippi

River valley. To the north, also on the Wisconsin side, is the village of Buffalo. The even smaller town of Alma, dwarfed by the Dairyland Power Cooperative electricity plant, is farther upriver. For a view of the bluff you are now on, visit the Buena Vista City Park above Alma, a walk that is described in my book *Great Wisconsin Walks.*

After another set of stairs, the second step off our hillside stairway is onto a rock outcrop that juts out into air. The view here is as panoramic and breathtaking as the first, but the sense of danger is more real and chilling. There's nothing below you but treetops, and these are a long way down. It's easy to be distracted by the scene around you, so be careful.

After ascending about 15 more feet up a dirt and grass path, you'll reach the last set of 57 steps leading to the summit. The bluff top is usually serene, except on a windy day when an approach to the bluff's edge can be dangerous. The view is remarkable. Besides what you've already seen to the north and east, you can now gaze southward. Note how Lock and Dam No. 5 cuts the river channel apart. If you're lucky or wait long enough, you'll see a barge, or several strung together, pushed by a hard-working river tug, maneuver into the lock and be lowered (or raised if going upriver) several feet. Also to the south are the other two bluffs, Hope, in the foreground, and Faith. You may not be able to easily discern them because, from this vantage point, they usually blend together. In the afternoon, however, when the bluffs begin to cast shadows eastward across Highway 61, you can distinctly see the shadows of each bluff. Also note the bluffs' bare rock outcrops, which once served as nesting sites for peregrine falcons. Although none have nested there for decades, it is hoped a pair will return as the population recovers from near extinction in the area.

The return hike is all downhill, literally. Enjoy it and the memories of spectacular bluff-top views.

Dakota to Meadow Trail
Whitewater State Park

Distance: 3 Miles

Time: 2 hours

Path: Mostly dirt, with some rocks and roots making footing tricky in spots. The stairs at the outset of the hike are steep and long, the decent down to the river crossing midway through the hike is difficult. The trail is well marked.

Directions: From the intersection of Highway 14 and Highway 74 in St. Charles, take Highway 74 north for 5 miles; the road bisects the park. For this hike, park in the lot of the nature store on the right side of the road about .5 mile into the park.

Contact: Whitewater State Park, Route 1, Box 256, Altura, MN 55910; (507)932-3007.

Highlights: There are several thrilling views of the Whitewater River and its valley from numerous overlooks set along sheer rock faces, plus some pulse-quickening vertical ascents and descents along the trail.

If it's important for you to limber up before a hike, you'd better do so before starting this one. You're going to climb approximately 160 vertical feet in only about 500 feet of hiking. The sign at the trailhead just across the road from the nature store says "Dakota Trail . . . Difficult." Actually, except for the initial climb to the top of the bluff and a tough decent in the middle, the hike isn't that hard. But that first climb is tough! Park officials have provided a well-built set of steps, with even rises and secure planking, yet the continuous grade is taxing. This is reason enough to take a break part way up and admire the picnic table made from stone or, a bit farther, to stop and cast an eye upward, toward the bare rock face that towers above, with hunks of it hanging precipitously over your head.

When the steps curve around the back of that rock face, you've nearly reached the top. But one more surprise awaits. The second-to-last group of stairs is called a "ladder," and it comes complete with a warning sign (a stick figure falling off backward!). The climb is steep, but handrails make you feel safer.

Once on top of the bluff, you'll be able to gaze directly across the river valley, over the top of the nature store. Only a few steps to the

129

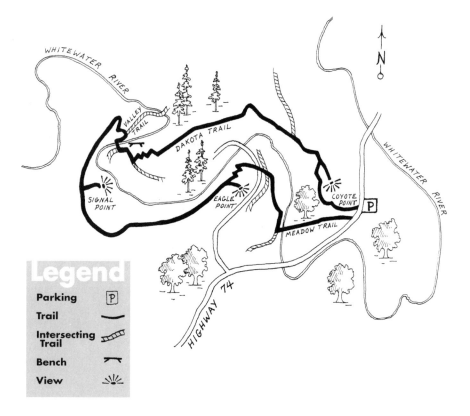

Legend

Parking	P
Trail	—
Intersecting Trail	
Bench	
View	

right is Coyote Point, which affords you another view up the river valley and up Highway 74. Catch your breath and then head back past the steps you just climbed and continue on the trail, which has about 20 more vertical feet to dish out before you gain the top of this bluff, which stands about 1,080 feet above sea level.

As the trail loops around the south side of the bluff, there are several short trails leading to valley overlooks. When you reach a junction where the Coyote Trail heads right, you should stay straight, or left, along the bluff. As you scramble across an eroded ravine, look uphill and see a jumble of fallen trees, which may help retard the erosion here.

From the ravine it's a short climb back up to the top of the bluff, where the trail hugs the south rim. As the crest of the bluff narrows, you'll soon see the river and its tight valley below you to the right. Enjoy the view because you'll then embark on a serious descent. The first half or so is steep and eroded, so watch you step on the tricky footing. When you reach a nude white pine, the tough part of the descent is over. *Nude* white pine? Well, it's dead and its bark has fallen away, exposing a rust-colored interior, especially where woodpeckers have excavated holes. Then, it's only another 100 yards to a junction with the Valley Trail. Turn right and in about 20 yards you'll find a bench along the bank of the Whitewater River. If you look upriver to the right, you can see the riverside bluff you just hiked down. White pine jut skyward from its steep rock sides.

The trail traces the riverbank for a few hundred feet before reaching a crossing made from large rectangular rock slabs set in the riverbed; the slabs are of Winona traviner, a locally quarried stone. Before crossing the river, note the milky sediment on the river bottom. This is light-colored clay from upriver and is how river got the name Whitewater. After crossing it, you'll hike for a short time through a floodplain filled with hackberry and small elm trees. When you reach a signboard, turn right and head back uphill. The trail is narrow and steep and provides an opportunity to tumble a long way down to the river on the left if you miss a step. It only climbs about halfway up the bluff, bare rock visible above.

At the next signboard, take a left and hike the 15 yards out to Signal Point. The river is directly below, and its rapids are quite audible. And right across the valley you can see the spine of the bluff and part of the descent you just traversed.

Back on the main trail, you'll hike away from the bluff's edge and negotiate a gradually sloping ravine, which renders the perfect amphitheater. What a place for a Pink Floyd concert! Once past the amphitheater, the trail hugs the edge of the bluff, from which a few rocky promontories jut over the river valley to the left. The park buildings are visible through the trees and seem almost directly below. One particularly dangerous overlook consists of a two-foot-square bare rock outcrop and a 10-foot-tall juniper that serves as a handhold. The parking lot lies below, as do the tops of sveral white pine.

The next stop is Eagle Point. Watch for signboard marking its location. Take the stairs to the right and then step out onto the bare rock. The view is mostly to the south and east, similar to the one you experienced at the beginning of the hike from Coyote Point, which you can now see quite well. When you return to the stairs and begin your walk down, look to the right to the sheer rock looming above you that comprises Eagle Point.

When you reach the park road, turn right and take it about 40 feet and then turn left into a mowed-grass area, where you'll come to a signboard for the Meadow Trail. Continue on this new trail, heading away from the park road, through a small thicket of pin cherry trees, toward the river and a suspension bridge. Cross the river, then trek through a wonderful stand of large black walnut and elm at the base of Coyote Point. You'll come to the end of this hike at the Dakota Trail sign you started from some time before.

Along Crystal-Clear Lakes

Blind Ash Bay Trail
Voyageurs National Park

Distance: 3 miles, round trip

Time: 2 hours

Path: This is a walk though woodlands and gullies and along steep hill-sides. While the path is not in itself difficult, an occasional fallen tree and other obstacles may impede your progress. Trail signs and other marking are absent. As in any wilderness hike, take some essential emergency supplies and a compass.

Directions: From the intersection of Highway 53 and County Highway 129 (Ash River Trail) about 25 miles southeast of International Falls, take 129 east for 8 miles to the intersection marked by a sign pointing left to the Ash River Visitor Center. Take that road, which ends at the visitor center, and park in the lot. Make sure you visit the center and talk to the personnel there about your intended hike, just to make sure you aren't surprised by a closed or wet trail.

Contact: Voyageurs National Park, 3131 Highway 53, International Falls, MN 56649; (218)283-9821.

Highlights: This is a trail into the wilderness. There are no roads: you're limited to traveling by water and foot in this region. Voyageurs is a giant water park. No, not the kind with slides and wave pools, but one where you can canoe for days and not leave the park. In fact, without a boat, you won't be able to see more than half of it, because it is isolated by the 30 lakes within its boundaries. On this hike, however, you can get a feel for the park without resorting to a boat. And at the far end of the trail, you'll see the results of a prescribed burn that got out of hand.

From the visitor center parking area, find the stairs that lead up to a second parking lot. When you reach these stairs that are just across the road that brought you here, make sure you turn around and look back at Kabetogama Lake. This is the first of many views you'll get of this giant body of water dotted by numerous islands.

After climbing the stairs, cross the upper parking lot toward the south and find the Blind Ash Bay River Trail. Then it's a steep 90-foot-climb up to the bluff top, along which the trail snakes for a short distance. All around you are various sized red pine, white spruce, white birch, and white pine, and along the trail edge you'll see blueberry and lots of big-leafed aster. Also, as you walk, you can get another glimpse of the big lake off to the right.

You'll soon pass a trail junction, as a trail from yet another parking lot joins the one you are on. Shortly afterwards, you'll encounter the first of several gullies, short, abrupt drops where the trail dips down into low spots. This time, you'll pass by and into a small stand of white cedar. The trail will ascend again, then descend into another low area, this one populated with black ash and aspen, and with thousands of ferns as ground cover.

Just when you think you're in the middle of the wild, you'll come upon a blacktop service road that leads to a Park Service garage. If you came here to get away from any vestige of civilization, don't get discouraged just cross the road and keep following the trail. Before moving on, note that magpie can be found in this area. These crow-sized birds have unique white and black markings and are noted for their raucous call and thieving habits.

Legend	
Parking	P
Trail	—
Park Office	🏠
Bench	⌒
Marsh	⅄

You should also begin to notice the fire scars at the base of many of the trees here. You'll see more and more evidence of the out-of-control burn mentioned earlier as you walk farther along the trail. You are now hiking through an aspen upland. But note one dead jack pine along the trail that really stands out as one hiker suggested, the cones decorating its limbs look like rosary beads, or perhaps plums. See if you agree.

Past the upland, the trail makes another dip, this time into a larger wet area full of spruce and black ash. The climb up the other side is steep, and the trail switches back once in order to better negotiate the steep incline. Not far from the switchback is a trail junction, formed by the trail looping back here. So, go right, follow the circle, you'll eventually return to this spot.

After turning right, you'll note that the woods have changed a bit and that you're surrounded by more upland trees, such as red oak and maple. Some of the oak are quite large. When you begin seeing lots of jack pine, you'll also see Kabetogama Lake again on the right. There are several lovely views of the lake along this path. When you reach a bench about halfway around the loop, you may want to sit awhile, take in the scene, and enjoy the solitude.

The trail past the bench loops left, and soon the water you see on the right is no longer the expanse of Kabetogama Lake but Blind Ash Bay, this trail's namesake. With its narrow entrance and mile-long size, it could well have provided a haven for early voyageurs seeking refuge from a storm.

The trail drops down near the shore of the bay though an almost pure stand of red pine, many of which carry now-familiar fire scars at their bases. When the trail turns away from the bay and begins climbing back up the slope, you'll see an acre-sized hole in the canopy of red pine near the top of the hill. Walk closer to see why. The trees here don't just have fire scars; they have been burned almost completely. All that remains are charred pieces of tree trunk on the ground. It seems that the "controlled burn" set back in 1994 got out of control and did the damage you see here. As you hike by the burn, look back at the bay for one last time. You'll then hike though a grove of white pine and come to the junction you passed going the other way. Bear right and retrace the route you took to get here, and you'll eventually return to the parking area.

Levee Walk
Zippel Bay State Park

Distance: 2 miles

Time: 1 hour

Path: The first half of this walk is along a beach, so the surface is sandy, sometimes soft, sometimes firm, depending on whether the level of the Lake of the Woods is high or low. The return trail is on an old road, most of which is covered by mowed grass. There are no markers of any consequence, but it would be difficult to get lost, since the trail is enclosed by the lake on one side, a wetland on the other, and a river beyond the turnaround point.

Directions: At the intersection of Highway 11 and County Highway 4, about 9 miles west of Baudette, take Highway 4 north to County Highway 8. Go west (left) on County 8 about 1 mile to County Highway 34; the park entrance is on the right.

Contact: Zippel Bay State Park, HC2, Box 25, Williams, MN 56686; (218)783-6252.

Highlights: Lake of the Woods is big water, and it sets the stage here. The lake amplifies the weather, and whatever the conditions, wind and rain, sun and heat, cold and snow, or anything in between, they are the highlight, along with the wonderful lake. You may see the remains of a big fish washed up on shore or sight a rare piping plover.

Start this walk from the parking area that serves the swimming beach and picnic area. Walk to the edge of Lake of the Woods and turn left up the beach. The loose and dunelike sand underfoot near the grassy, shrubby margin of the shore makes for difficult walking. Hike down near the water, where the sand is harder and makes for easier treading.

What you hear and see and smell out here will largely depend on the lake's mood. A calm day or a south wind favors subtle things, like the sound of gulls calling to one another, the sight of millions of lake-washed stones along the water's edge, or the fragrance of terrestrial things, like grasses, trees, and dirt. If the day is windy, especially if the wind is from the north or northeast, you'll be overwhelmed by the lake itself: its power, its enormity, its wild beauty.

In the midst of all this, you may want to ponder a few facts about the scene before you. The lake covers 1,695 square miles, making it the largest body of water accessible from Minnesota (with the exception of Lake Superior, of course, which is always in a class by itself). From the shore you are on, it is 80 miles to the northern tip of the lake, located in Ontario, Canada. You can't see any other land offshore from your vantage point, but out there somewhere are 14,000 islands. The park brochure claims that the lake has 65,000 miles of shoreline (including the islands). Yet the lake has a maximum depth of only 69 feet! (Lake Superior sounds in at 1,333 feet.)

Unless the wind is fierce and pushes the water way up unto the beach, you'll notice lots of clam shells in the sand. Gulls bring them here, as does the surf. There are also lots of pea-sized stones, round and smooth from the water's constant rolling.

As you walk toward the point that juts out into the lake, you may spy some shorebirds, plover or terns, pecking around in the sheltered, shallow bay. Zippel Bay is one of only four

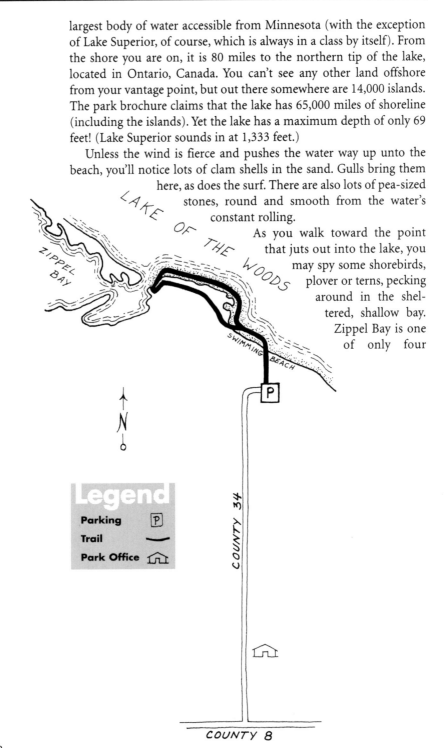

breeding areas on the lake for the endangered piping plover, and there are only 25 breeding pairs on the entire lake. As you walk along the beach, you'll undoubtedly disturb a flock of gulls that always sit near the point.

As you round the point, you'll see a jetty with a navigation light located at its lakeward end. The levee and adjacent jetty stabilize the entrance to Zippel Bay. They were created in 1986 so that the channel into the bay didn't change drastically with every major storm. As you walk toward the jetty, continue your beachcombing. Dead fish often wash up here and make for interesting discoveries. Since the Lake of the Woods is home to one of the best northern pike fisheries around, you might find a 35-inch pike. Other fish in the lake are walleye, smallmouth bass, perch, muskie, and the less-common lake sturgeon. Sturgeon here may reach 100 years of age and weigh over 250 pounds! In fact, the mouth of Zippel Bay was home to a thriving commercial sturgeon-processing plant back in the early 1900s.

When you reach the jetty and levee, head inland a bit along the jetty's rock edge until you're able to walk across the sand near the shore at the mouth of the bay. There are a variety of birds here taking advantage of the shelter. Among them is the double-crested cormorant, a large awkward-looking, ducklike bird. If you're very lucky, you'll see some white pelicans, sporting strange pouched beaks.

Walk farther up the beach, along the bay's inlet, to where you will be stymied by marsh and cattails. Here you can look up the bay across acres of marshland. Ducks fly here in the morning and near sunset. And the rattling, raspy call of sandhill cranes can often be heard in the distance.

Then walk back up the inlet beach and reenter the trail near some large boulders. Follow the mowed path, which moves along a small rise that parallels the beach you walked on earlier. With vegetation on each side, the rise actually marks one of the lake's earlier shorelines. There are many of these throughout the park, evidence that the lake has risen and fallen many times over the past 10,000 years.

As you hike down this road-wide path, mostly covered with grass but also with plenty of loose sand, you'll note the large wetland to the right. Dryland plants such as box elder, elm, balsam poplar, grapevines, and grasses occupy this little linear bump you are walking along. Birds love it also. There are lots of robins, plus chipping sparrows and an occasional blue jay. You may also see some clam shells along the path, most likely brought here by raccoons, who feasted on the contents.

The old lakeshore path ends at the beach that you traversed earlier. After your exit, keep walking; the parking lot is about 100 yards up and to the right.

Pine Ridge Interpretive Trail and Dam Walk
Hayes Lake State Park

Distance: 2 miles, round trip

Time: 1 hour

Path: The walk is along and near the lakeshore over a mowed grass path and though a mowed picnic area. There are numbered stations along the first part of the trail and an interpretative brochure that talks about them. This is an easy walk.

Directions: From the intersection of Highways 89, 11, and 310 in Roseau, take 89 south approximately 14.5 miles to County Highway 4. Turn left (east) on County 4 for 8 miles to the park entrance on the right.

Contact: Hayes Lake State Park, 48990 County Road 4, Roseau, MN 56751; (218)425-7504.

Highlights: This is a pleasant, easy amble along the banks of an interesting artificial lake. Both on your initial walk and on your walk back, watch for signs of beaver activity, which are everywhere, and for an old jack pine skeleton that stands like an organic sculpture along the trail.

Start your walk where the Pine Ridge Trail crosses through the campground next to campsite number 15. The path here is white gravel but soon changes to mowed grass. On your right is a white spruce plantation. Planted in 1970, these trees have grown rapidly for such a northern site. They are planted very close together, about four feet apart in rows about six feet apart. The furrows in which they were planted help them retain moisture and give them a bit of an advantage in the dry, sandy soil.

The path soon enters an opening that affords you your first good look at Hayes Lake, which is not very wide and occupies an old river bed. Beaver activity is sometimes evident along this section of trail. Look for downed aspen or sharp, pointed stumps.

Soon the trail enters another plantation, this one of red pine, also called Norway pine. Native to the upper Midwest, red pine are often grown in plantations because they grow fast and are fairly pest-free. One drawback is that they shade out every other plant, creating a monoculture, a one-species woodland. This lack of diversity is detrimental to wildlife because it provides little habitat and is a poor food source.

The path through the plantation is needle covered and very cushioned. When it exits the red pine it enters a little chokecherry thicket. These trees are valuable for wildlife because they produce abundant, large, dark purple fruit that birds love. Bears also like the fruit, as evidenced by the occasional bent and broken tree stems ripped down to eating level by the hungry creatures.

As you progress down the trail, you'll pass the skeleton of a short and gnarly jack pine on the right. Pine cones, looking like dark plums, still cling to its branches. Several rows of planted jack pine are visible on the left side of the trail just before you reach a bench and a sign that marks Beauty Bay, a small indentation on the shoreline of Hayes Lake.

Then it's back into red pine again. The bareness of the understory is striking. Once you reach the next opening, it's only a few hundred feet until you reach the picnic grounds and beach area. There's drinking water available here. Continue across the picnic area, past the parking lot, and pick up the mowed trail again as it loops gently left along the lakeshore. Look for the several small (3- to 5-inch-diameter) hackberry on the left. These trees, identifiable by their ridged,

corky-looking bark, are a surprising find so far north. They make their best farther south, along the Mississippi River between Minnesota and Wisconsin.

Additional signs of beaver handiwork are all over this area, especially lots of stumps and mashed-down vegetation along the lake. Unlike some beaver, these fellows live in holes and caverns along the bank. Since the concrete dam was constructed at the far end of the lake, most of their tree felling has been for food, not building materials.

Hike past the dock and canoe landing, across the mowed area dotted with picnic tables, and around to the large signboard telling about the dam that formed Hayes Lake in 1971, four years after the area was designated as a state park. The dam was built because there wasn't much water-related recreation in the area, an idea advocated by A. F. Hayes, whose family settled the area. The dam is just ahead, beyond the signboard.

One problem with the lake after its development was low oxygen levels. Lots of decaying matter in the lake, combined with thick snow cover on the ice in the winter, caused oxygen levels in the lake to plummet in late winter and early spring. Fish suffered and many died. The solution, which is discussed and illustrated on the signboard, was to extend the outflow pipe. This pipe, which draws water from the bottom of the lake and expels it below the dam, was extended from near the top of the dam to near the middle of the lake, thereby pulling oxygen-rich water from near the surface into the oxygen-depleted areas deeper in the lake. The problem was solved, much to the pleasure of the area anglers and the fish.

Walk out onto the dam and look around. You'll see the Moose Ridge Trail crossing the dam but not crossing back over the river. Since the trail is over 4 miles long one way, be ready for a long hike if you choose it. Otherwise, turn around and retrace your steps back to your vehicle.

Bjorkland Lake Hike
Lake Maria State Park

Distance: 2 miles

Time: 1 hour

Path: Gravel and dirt make up the surface of most of the trail, which also has some sections of mowed grass. The trail is well marked, with signboards at intersections. This trek is full of hills, some of which are steep.

Directions: From Monticello, take County Highway 39 approximately 6 miles west to County Highway 111. Go north(right)on County 111 for approximately .5 mile to the park entrance on the left.

Contact: Lake Maria("Ma-rye-uh")State Park, 11411 Clementa Ave. N. W., Monticello, MN 55362; (612)878-2325.

Highlights: This hike offers some challenging hills and a view of a prairie pothole lake surrounded by wetlands. There are lots of waterfowl near the lake in spring and fall.

Start this walk from the parking lot near the trail center building. Find the trail just west of the lot and head right, toward the trail center. As you approach the center, note the solar-powered, low-voltage lights atop 2-foot-high lightposts. Constructed in 1978, part of the structure is set in a berm for a low, unobtrusive appearance and energy efficiency.

Just west of the trail center you'll arrive at a couple of trailheads and some map boards. Find the trail that leads to campsites B7 and B8 and begin your hike. As you start, you'll see an almost pure stand of ironwood, and if you look closer, you'll see that white oak grow here too, forming a tall canopy over the tops of the shade tolerant ironwood.

As the trail drops gradually downhill, the ironwood thin out, and the white oak get bigger and are joined by red oak. Many of the red oak are dead, bark sloughed off, large limbs broken and lying on the ground. The two-lined chestnut borer struck this stand, and red oak all over the park are suffering from this insect, which tunnels into trees and girdles them. Normally the borer doesn't inflict this much damage, but this infestation followed the drought of 1988 and 1989, with a lot of red oak mortality the result.

As you progress a series of roller-coaster hills, you'll notice several low wet areas at the bottom of the larger hills. The same glacier that created the hills created these potholes. Big hunks of ice were sitting in these holes 10,000 years ago. The ice melted and left the depressions you see today.

After descending a hill so steep you almost have to run down it, you'll come to a junction with a map board and a bench. Campsite B7 is off to the right. You'll want to continue left, toward Bjorkland Lake. On the way, you'll see a deep, wide ravine on the left and an open plain on the right. The area you're treading on is an esker, a ridge created thousands of years ago by a river of meltwater running below glacial ice. Look at the sandy and pebbly soil. The absence of large rocks and boulders tells you that it was deposited by water.

When you reach Bjorkland Lake, walk down to the wooden platform that overlooks this nearly round body of water. Bjorkland is a prairie pothole lake, one created by the same glacier that left its imprint on so many other parts of the region. There are thousands of such lakes in Minnesota, many of them in an arc stretching hundreds of miles from here to the northwest.

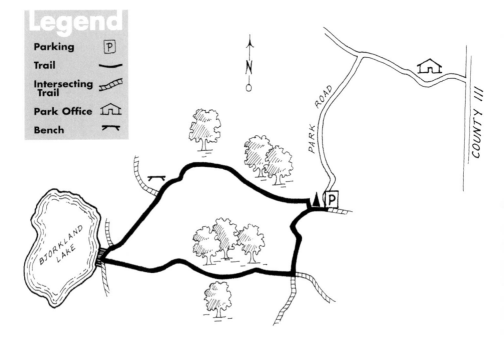

If you look directly across the lake from the platform, you may be able to see a cone-shaped landform about two acres in size and covered with oak trees. It stands out because the rest of the shore of this lake is all flat wetland. It is likely that this cone is a kame, formed when water seeped through the glacier carrying sand and silt and depositing them in a pile that became this tree-covered hill.

When you're ready, begin the hike back to the parking area by locating the map board and heading out to the left of it, with the lake to your back. You'll traverse a grassy field and then enter some woods. You'll pass a half-acre pond on the right, then climb a bit, passing several backpack-camping sites. At one point, you'll walk through an almost pure-white stand of oak, with ghostlike, dusty-white trunks, 8 to 18 inches in diameter. In the late fall, dry, brown leaves clinging stubbornly to gnarly branches will whisper in the cold breeze as they wait for winter's white coat. Farther down the trail, an 8-point buck may jump across the trail and disappear into a tangle of fallen red oak tops and brambles.

When you reach the next junction, go left. Soon you'll see the ironwood again, along with white oak. This is a sign you're back at the beginning of the hike. When you can see the trail center, the parking area and your vehicle will be off to the right.

Big Island Trail
Myre-Big Island State Park

Distance: 1.5 miles

Time: 1 hour

Path: Asphalt and worn dirt.

Directions: From the intersection of I-35 and County Highway 46 just east of Albert Lea, take Highway 46 east for .5 mile to County Highway 38. Turn right and go south. It's .5 mile to the park entrance. Take the park road to the parking area on Big Island near the campground.

Contact: Myre-Big Island State Park, Route 3, Box 33, Albert Lea, MN 56007; (507)379-3403.

Highlights: A forest of big trees sitting on a 116-acre patch of land in the middle of 2,600-acre Albert Lea Lake is the setting for this easy hike that circles the island.

Big Island is actually a peninsula, thanks to a road that was built in the 1940s linking the area with the "mainland." The northern hardwood forest that occupies the island is not a common sight in this part of Minnesota. Because of its location in the lake, the island was protected from fires that swept the region prior to white settlement. Hence trees other than the fire resistant bur oak thrived here in fertile, moist soil. Wildflowers on the island are typical of damp northern forests: bloodroot, hepatica, wild ginger, spring beauty, Dutchman's breeches, and trout lily. There is also plenty of cutweed and poison ivy, so don't go prancing off trail in your shorts.

Park at the northeast end of the parking lot by the interpretive center. Take the asphalt path that leads into a grove of sugar maples, hackberry, and black walnut. An experienced tree-lover will be surprised, even confused, by the variation of the bark, especially on the maples. Something about the growth rate, soil, and/or moisture here causes maple bark to vary in texture.

It's a short walk to a spot with benches and a podium used for outdoor education by the park staff. Beyond this, the path becomes dirt and can be muddy. You'll pass a giant basswood tree about 10 yards into the woods on the right before reaching a junction. Take the trail that heads left, out onto a little grassy point of land jutting into the lake that affords a view of tranquil farm fields on the opposite shore. But the gentle slope of those fields down to the water is actually contributing to the lake's environmental crisis. Agricultural runoff is accelerating the natural eutrophic process of this shallow glacial lake; and algae blooms, common in the summer, color the water a pea green.

Head back to the main trail and continue your circle of the island. You'll pass some magnificent large old trees, including a 3-foot-diameter hackberry next to the trail on the left.

When you reach a junction and signboard, stay left to curve around the south end of the island. At the junction, to the left of the

Legend

Parking	P
Trail	—
Intersecting Trail	

N

ALBERT LEA LAKE

COUNTY 38

INTERPRETIVE CENTER

ALBERT LEA LAKE

trail, you'll see an uncommonly large ironwood tree *(Ostrya virginiana),* also called hop hornbeam. This giant is a foot in diameter and over 50 feet tall, one of the biggest such trees in Minnesota. It's called ironwood because its dense and heavy wood is unusually tough, resisting nails and sawteeth. Because its denseness makes it resistant to rot, the wood is often used for fence posts.

When you reach the next junction and signboard, turn left and head out on a long, narrow strip of land. Cottonwood and willow dominate here, where the water is closer and the soil wetter. There are lots of wind-thrown trees too, because the point is exposed to serious winds. On your way back to the main trail, look at the trees on the island ahead of you. They present a tall green wall that towers over the shoreline.

When you reach the junction, turn left and continue down the trail to the next signboard and road. Turn right onto the road and hike past campsite 23 to campsite 26, where you can pick up an asphalt trail, one of three loops comprising an accessible trail system designed to accommodate handicapped individuals. Any of these loops leads back through the center of the island to the interpretive center. The woods along these paths is a jungle of vines, shrubs, smaller trees and plenty of poison ivy. So stay on the trail. Once at the interpretive center, the parking lot and your vehicle are nearby to the north.

Wilderness Trails

Eagle Mountain Trail
Superior National Forest/Boundary Waters Canoe Area Wilderness

Distance: 7 miles, round trip

Time: 3 to 4 hours

Path: Wow! Although this path begins on crushed rock, don't be fooled. Within a few hundred yards it becomes strewn with boulders and crisscrossed with roots. It's doubtful that even a short person could lie down on any portion of this trail without having some part of his or her body touch either a rock or a root. The rocks and boulders are of such varied size and so abundant that on sections of the trail it's difficult to find a place for one's foot. Indeed, placing a foot on a rock is often the only choice. Although the trail ends at the highest point in Minnesota, most of the climb occurs in the last .5 mile and, although taxing, is not too difficult. Actually, climbing a trail littered with rocks is easier than walking over the same types of rocks on a level surface.

Directions: From Grand Marais, take the Gunflint Trail (County Highway 12) 4 miles north to County Highway 8. Go left for 5 miles on 8 to County Road 27; go right on 27 for another 5 miles to Forest Road 170, then left. The parking area and trailhead map board are on the right. Registration is required even for day hikes. Self-registration forms are in a box attached to the map board. If you're planing an overnight stay, a permit is required, which can be obtained in Grand Marais or at any other of the many Superior National Forest offices along the north shore of Lake Superior.

Contact: Forest Supervisor, Superior National Forest, P.O. Box 338, Duluth, MN 55801; (218)626-4300 and (218)720-5433 TTY; or Gunflint Ranger District, P.O. Box 790, Grand Marais, MN 55604; (218)387-1750.

Highlights: This hike ventures into one of the largest, most enthralling wildernesses in the eastern half of the United States. There are terrific views of a wilderness lake and a fabulous view from the top of the highest point in Minnesota.

A difficult path often leads to a reward, and this hike certainly does. Also, there are a couple of other positive stimuli along the trail on the way to the reward. The trail's first third of a mile or so gently undulates through a forest of jack pine, aspen, and balsam fir. Lichen, often hanging down several inches and looking like moss, clings to dead and live pine branches.

The first break in the woods is a small clearing on the left. It's filled with grasses and sedges that can tolerate the wet, shady, low area. Around the edge of the clearing, willows compete for sunlight with meadowsweet, red-twig dogwood, and hazelnut.

Then you'll cross a small bog on planks that someone has lugged a long way. Once across, you'll see the Boundary Waters Canoe Area sign that reads "Closed to Motorized Vehicles and Motorized Equipment." Those last two words refer to, among other dubious inventions of modern civilization, chain saws. But it will be a while before such equipment will be needed again: the area was logged, along with the rest of northern Minnesota, back in the early 1900s.

About 50 minutes into your hike, you will enter a vast open area on a plank walk that's over 100 yards long. Here, you can gaze at the surrounding ridges, including the bottom of Eagle Mountain off to the northwest. On the ground near the plank walk, look for moose prints in the wet soil; they browse the alder along the walkway. If you're lucky and actually see a moose, make sure you give it plenty of room. Moose can be dangerous. And if you encounter a cow with a calf, give them even more room and never get between mom and her kid.

Farther up the trail, a wilderness lake awaits. As you emerge from the woods on the shore of Whale Lake, be prepared the view can take your breath away. Along the opposite shoreline, cedar trees in dense conical shapes form a background for the incredibly intense blue water. Reaching above the cedar, sharp-tipped balsam fir poke into the deciduous woods blanketing the hillside behind the lake. Various textures and shapes and more shades of green than imaginable mingle between the azure lake and the blue sky.

Enjoy the view here because the trail ahead, which hugs the lakeshore, is rugged and full of boulders, which requires that you divide viewing and walking into two separate activities. Plus, the dense cedar along the trail block any expansive views. Also, notice the cedar seedlings growing near the trail. These are unusual because white-tailed deer have so overpopulated many northern habitats that they destroy small cedars before the trees can grow for more than a season or two.

When you reach the trail sign with an arrow that points to Eagle Mountain, take a deep breath and get ready: the real climbing is about

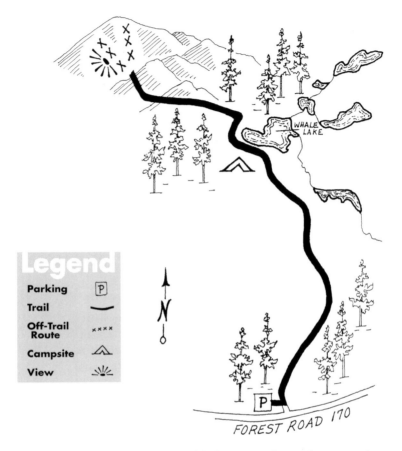

Legend

Parking	P
Trail	—
Off-Trail Route	x x x x
Campsite	⌂
View	☀

N

WHALE LAKE

FOREST ROAD 170

to begin. Big rocks and little ones make good steps up the steep hill-side. Then the trail surface becomes mostly giant granite slabs, part of the bedrock that comprises this mountain. Trees are now smaller because they have a tough time growing on granite. There's a view to the left. It's through the trees initially, but an opening ahead affords a view of the flat plain below and the rippling ridges beyond.

Keep climbing, the best is still ahead. The trail comes upon yet another expanse of bare granite. But before you indulge in the view off to the left, make sure you actually get to the top of this rock for-mation. Look hard and you'll see that the trail continues to the right. Look for tree roots that have the typical look of being worn down by hundreds of footfalls. The path takes you back into the shrubby woods and loops farther right to a spot where you'll see a large plaque put there by the Minnesota Historical Society in 1969. This is the summit of Eagle Mountain, the highest point in Minnesota, 2,301 feet above sea level and approximately 1,700 feet above Lake Superior.

Now it's time for the view. Head back out of the woods the way you just came, then down the bare granite. You'll reach the edge of the hill, with an almost sheer drop below. To the south you'll see a couple of lakes right below the mountain. The one on the left is Shrike Lake, and the one on the immediate right is Zoo Lake. If you strain your neck a bit, Eagle Lake is visible on the far right. Farther south you'll see a ribbon of openings disconnected by the forest. This is the North Branch of the Cascade River. Also, on a clear day, Lake Superior is visible on the horizon, in the low spots between curved ridges. Sometimes, especially with the aid of binoculars, you can see ore ships out on the water.

When you've seen enough, retrace your steps down the mountain. And make sure you look back at Whale Lake as you pass it. The light will have changed, and thus the view will be different, even though nothing else in the scene will have moved. Monet taught us that about light. But even he'd have trouble capturing the colors and shapes of this wilderness lake.

Bass Lake Trail
Superior National Forest

Distance: 6 miles

Time: 4 hours

Path: Mostly unimproved, except for some wood plank walkways over wet areas. There are lots of various-sized rocks, some wind-toppled trees, and plenty of ups and downs that, together with the area's general ruggedness, make this a difficult hike.

Directions: From the intersection of Highway 169 and County Highway 88 just east of Ely, take County 88 north 2 miles to the Echo Trail(County Highway 116). Proceed on the Echo Trail for 4 miles; the parking area and trailhead are on the right.

Contact: Forest Supervisor, Superior National Forest, P.O. Box 338, Duluth, MN 55801; (218)626-4300 and(218)720-5433 TTY; or Gunflint Ranger District, P.O. Box 790, Grand Marais, MN 55604; (218)387-1750.

Highlights: Bodies of water the size of Bass Lake don't drop 60 feet in 24 hours very often. This hike takes you around the lake, which experienced such a drop and did it in the recent past. The area is remote, rugged, and wild. Striking vistas are common and wildlife is everywhere.

In April 1925, Bass Lake was the site of a disaster of momentous proportions. Over a billion and a half cubic feet of water broke through a gravel ridge that had blocked the lake's outlet and rushed into Low Lake and beyond. In a couple of hours, Bass Lake's level was reduced by 60 feet! The disaster was only "seminatural" because a logging operation had altered the gravel ridge some years before in order to move logs from Bass to Low Lake. This hike takes you out to the area of the former gravel ridge and along some of the old lake bottom.

Start your hike at the parking area, where a signboard tells you about the washout, and head right at the first junction. A left turn takes you to Dry Falls, which you will see toward the end of this hike. Once you reach Bass Lake, your first sight of it is impressive. Across the narrow end of the lake here, a tree-crowned knob of granite immediately demands your attention. Such stark granite outcrops are the norm around this lowered lake but unusual anywhere else.

From this close approach to the lake, you'll climb a hillside that runs the entire 1.5-mile length of the lake. The trail will cross an occasional ravine that takes you down toward the lake but never right to its shore. Three distinct groups of trees layer the hillside. White birch grow from the water's edge up about 50 feet. Smaller white pine and balsam fir have seeded in and are growing beneath the birch. This is the area that was exposed when the lake level dropped in 1925. White cedar grow on the steepest slopes, along the middle of the hillside, and approach the top. Larger red and white pine occupy the well-drained windswept top of the ridge.

About halfway along the length of the lake, there's a steep 40-yard climb up some granite outcrops to a red-pine-covered vista. The 100-foot drop to the lake is abrupt, so be careful. Look back along the shoreline toward where you've been; you can see the bare granite cliff face that you glimpsed when you first came upon the lake. Directly across the narrow lake here is an island. Note how all its trees are about the same size. Before the catastrophe that dropped the water level, this island was underwater.

Back on the trail, you'll see a deep ravine to your right, then another slightly higher ridge beyond, which is topped by some impressive pine and spruce. Hobo Lake lies on the other side of this higher ridge. Many of the lakes here near Ely generally run in a north-easterly-southwesterly direction. The reason is that the bedrock, formed over a billion years ago, has faulted in this direction. Recent glaciers (about 15,000 years old) and more ancient ones have also left their mark, scouring out the lake beds and depositing massive gravel ridges like the one that once blocked the outlet of Bass Lake.

The descent down to lake level is gradual. On the way down, you can see a couple of red maple trees and some red-twig dogwood, neither of which grew up on the hillside because they like moist soil. A bridge provides you with a dry crossing of a small stream, a remnant of the torrent of water that carved this valley in 1925. Beaver-chewed tree stumps dot the low area beyond the bridge. At this point, you'll see Low Lake to your right as you hike out and loop back on a gravely spit of land, which was created when the water washed through here from Bass Lake. With Low Lake on your right, you'll hike on this spit for a quarter mile or so. There's a box toilet and campsite on your left. Shortly before the trail climbs up another ridge, you'll pass a steep slope of loose gravel, all that remains of the old gravel ridge that washed out. Try to picture the surface of Bass Lake, which you can see ahead of you, 60 feet higher than now. Imagine the roar of the water as it broke thought the gravel ridge and exploded down the valley toward Low Lake. In 1925, residents of Ely, four crow-fly miles away, heard it.

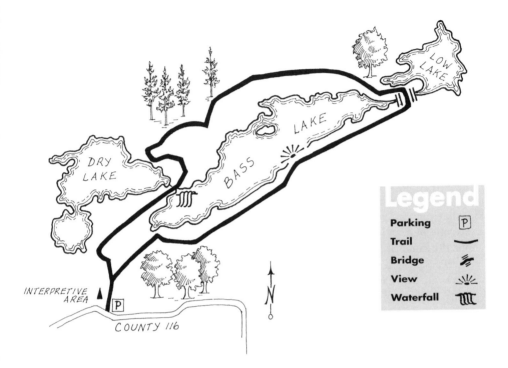

The climb up to the ridge above Bass Lake is gradual and comfortable; you are now on the opposite side of the lake. The old shoreline is visible on your right as a flat area above a rock cairn that marks the trail. A couple of older red pine grow on what would have been the old lakeshore. As you hike above the old shoreline, you'll head inland from the lake. A timber bridge crosses a 20-foot-deep ravine and leads to a stand of small birch and aspen. A forest fire that swept through here in the mid-1980s, created the fire scars that can be seen on the bases of some of the red pines. Today, moose like this area. Look in the softer, deeper soil of the ravines for prints. Or maybe you'll find some moose pellets along the trail. Anyone who's seen deer droppings will recognize moose scat and marvel at the size!

Your next view of Bass Lake is from a granite outcrop about halfway back to the southwest end of the lake. Although several hundred yards away from the lakeshore, you'll be able to see back toward where the gravel dam used to be. Interestingly, the little island that was visible from the other vista has disappeared from view here. It's actually tucked away, close to the western lake shore, right below you.

A series of at least 14 rock cairns guides you across a quarter mile or so of super-sized granite slabs. The trail then makes a steep descent off the slabs and into pine woods, with an almost 180-degree swing back to the left. The reason the trail alters course is Dry Lake up ahead. Several hundred feet after the trail doglegs to the left, watch on your left for a bearing tree (a tree that marks important survey corners). There is also a U.S. Geological Survey sign on a metal post sticking out of the ground. It was installed on December 5, 1985, and marks township 63, range 12, section 10.

A trail junction appears not far beyond the survey marker. The trail to the right goes about 100 feet to Dry Lake and is used primarily by canoeists. The trail to the left leads to a couple of primitive camp-sites on Bass Lake. You should keep straight ahead; you'll have only a 200-yard walk to Dry Falls. A bridge spans the small creek that tumbles from Dry Lake into Bass Lake. There are waterfalls below the bridge, and they require climbing some rock if you want to see them. This entire area was under 30 feet of water before the gravel dam broke. Across the bridge, you'll get another view of the falls from some rocks that jut into the lake.

The rest of the trail crosses more huge rock outcrops, dips into a couple of small ravines, and parallels the deep ravine that used to be the southwestern end of Bass Lake. The path then drops into the old lake bed. After climbing out of the it, you'll connect with the trail that brought you here. Make a right turn; the parking lot is less than a quarter mile away.

Herriman Trail
Superior National
Forest/Boundary Waters Canoe
Area Wilderness

Distance: 6 miles

Time: 3 hours

Path: This is a difficult hike. Although there is a definite trail along most of the way, you'll need to stay alert and sometimes determine exactly where the trail is. Fallen trees frequently cross the trail, and there are a couple of very wet areas. Trail marking is inconsistent. Make sure you have a compass and other emergency gear.

Directions: From the junction of County Highway 24 and County Road 424, 4 miles south of Crane Lake, take County 24 east and north for approximately 2 miles to the parking area on the left. The trailhead is on the right.

Contact: Superior National Forest, LaCroix Ranger District, 320 N. Highway 53, Cook, MN 55723; (218)666-0020.

Highlights: This is a walk in the wilderness. Perhaps the most impressive part of the walk are the massive granite slabs that lie on the east side of Herriman Lake. Conveniently enough, they seem to appear at about the time you're ready for a break, and they make wonderful places to sit or lie on while gazing at the lake.

This hike begins with a climb. From the road, you'll ascend for a couple of hundred yards up a fairly steep hill and through a cutover woods, until you reach a signboard and registration station. All trips into the Boundary Waters Canoe Area Wilderness (BWCAW) require you to fill out a small slip of paper with some details. You should do so (if for no other reason than to make sure the bureaucrats know someone is using these trails), then head off down the trail. Early on, you'll stroll over some plank walks and then pass a couple of large white spruce before heading downhill to a picnic area and the Echo River. As most rivers in far northern Minnesota, this one contains more rock than river, especially during dry times. But the granite slabs are impressive, even without much water. Cross the bridge and hike up the opposite bank. In about 15 yards you'll find a trail to the right.

This trail follows the Echo River upstream, and most of the impressive scenery is on the other side, which is predominated by tall white pine sticking out above the canopy. There are also some big pine on this side, in addition to aspen, ash, and other varieties of trees. In some years the ferns are chest high and the tangle of vegetation can be forbidding, especially if the area is wet from dew or rain. The trail will take you down into several small wet areas. Alder in some of them all but obscure the trail. Be careful here so that you don't lose the trail. The abundant white spruce here are notable because of the lichen that hangs from their branches, sometimes looking more like moss on a southern pine.

When the trail curves left, away from the river, pay close attention. You are near a junction, which is unmarked. You'll want to turn left and continue on away from the river. You'll hike uphill for a couple of hundred yards, then head back down to an wet area. This is the most confusing part of the trail. You'll want to continue in an easterly direction away from the river. You'll then come upon an old beaver dam.

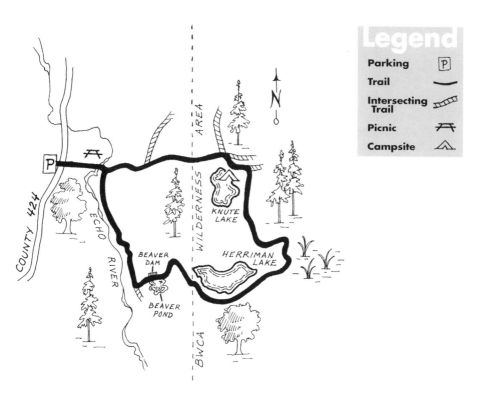

This is the easiest way across the water. Above the dam, farther right, is a pond full of lily pads.

Once across the dam, continue uphill, then along a hillside that's covered with balsam poplar. You'll soon encounter the trail's first knob of granite, covered with green to brown lichen. There are plenty of bunchberry, club mosses, and blue beadlilies too. Then you'll see the first of many stone cairns. These will help you cross large expanses of granite that don't have a visible path.

Soon after the first cairn you'll see a sign announcing the entrance to the BWCAW. As you hike, look to the left for swatches of blue peeking from between the trees; this is Herriman Lake. There are several scenic overlooks as you proceed along the south and east sides of the lake. Any one of these is a great place for a break, a stretch, and perhaps something to eat. The flat granite rock slabs are really quite comfortable.

As you continue, you'll leave Herriman Lake and the rock slabs behind and enter a woods full of big red oak and some white pine. As the trail dips down into a deep ravine, you'll pick your way across its bottom on huge boulders. There is an expansive wetland on the right, and the trail crosses the ravine before it opens into the wetland. You'll climb again, this time into an impressive grove of giant white pine.

Here, suddenly, the trees are short and stubby, with red oak beginning to predominate. This is the trail's highest point: a vast field of granite slabs with little vegetation. You'll walk on top of this rock dome for about 10 minutes. Make sure you look for the rock cairns. They really do help define the trail here, and without them you could get lost.

When the trail heads downhill, it's just a short walk until the woods begin again, and then not much longer until you can see the blue water of Knute Lake ahead. When you reach a junction, bear left toward the lake. Within a few hundred feet there's another junction, this one with a short 50-yard-long spur trail that takes you to a campsite on Knute Lake. It's worth the short detour. The lake is a gem: sparkling crystal-clear water ringed by balsam fir spires.

Back on the main trail, head left (west). You'll soon pass a path that cuts off to the right (north) toward Dovre Lake. The main trail then crosses a couple of wet areas and enters a deep, dark spruce woods as it exits the BWCAW. You'll pass a large open bog on the right. Gradually, the trail gets wider and more roadlike. After some more wetlands on the right, another trail from Dovre Lake enters from the right.

In less than a quarter mile, you'll be back to the Echo River and the bridge you crossed at the beginning of this hike.

Of Geologic Interest

Shovel Point and Beach Trails
Tettegouche State Park

Distance: 1.5 miles

Time: 1 hour

Path: Mostly dirt and bedrock. There is considerable climbing involved, with approximately 15 sets of stairs that must be negotiated twice, on the way out and the way back.

Directions: From Silver Bay take Highway 61 northeast 4.5 miles to the Tettegouche State Park entrance on the right at milepost 58.5.

Contact: Tettegouche State Park, 5702 Highway 61, Silver Bay, MN 55614; (218)226-6365.

Highlights: Rocks, lots of them, not to mention getting close-up and personal with the earth's largest lake.

We begin this hike from the information center at the park entrance. Walk toward Lake Superior out a broad, inviting concrete sidewalk. When you soon come to an elaborate sundial on your left, take a moment and read about it on the signboard nearby. The walkway ends at an overlook of the lake, where a large signboard illustrates the path to our destination, Shovel Point. Go left and you'll walk around a large two-foot-diameter white spruce, down a couple of sections of stairs to another sign, this one wooden with routed letters. On it one arrow points right, to the beach, and one left, to Shovel Point. Go left for now, we'll get to the beach on the way back.

The path winds through some large birch, probably gray birch not white. There are also mountain ash, alder, hazelnut, and mountain maple (also called moose maple). Most of these trees have been heavily browsed by deer and moose. Each winter the newest growth is chewed off, and each spring new branches extend upward, only to be eaten the next winter.

The first spectacular view comes just before and at a seven-sided wood viewing platform built along the trail. Directly below lies a cove, a concave sweep in the rocky shoreline and part of the beach we will visit on our way back. Beyond the cove to the southwest is the large, hulking mass of what's called Palisade Head. Both Palisade Head and Shovel Point are what geologists call sills, places where newer igneous rock has intruded into older rock, in this case basalt. These two sills are composed of porphyritic rhyolite. Porphyritic refers to the light-colored crystals of quartz and feldspar contained in the rocks. Rhyolite is a fine-grained igneous rock that has a reddish tinge. Since the older basalt in these sills is a bit softer, it erodes more quickly, leaving these wonderful examples of very long-term erosion (hundreds of millions of years).

Back on the trail, as you round the next bend, there's a good view of Shovel Point ahead, jutting out over the lake. Note how it slopes gradually downward and toward the southeast. To get there, you first have to climb several sets of stairs and root steps. The last set of 32 stair steps ends near another multisided wood platform. And what a view! The Lake Superior shoreline stretches off south and west. Palisade Head is dominant, but the mountainous inland park is also visible. More diminutive but most impressive is a small arch in the rock. Situated at the tip of one of many points jutting out into the lake, this arch is delicate, although it's probably big enough to pilot a yacht through. The mouth of the Baptism River is also visible but difficult to see because of the angle and the high rock cliffs on both sides. Unfortunately, the taconite mining complex in Silver Bay also makes its presence known both visibly, by way of a tower and some smoke, and audibly, via a constant and deep industrial hum.

The next part of this hike takes us out to the point's end in Lake Superior. After walking past the signboard that lies just beyond the wooden platform, traverse the large flat rock face, staying right, near the lake. The path takes you through a sparsely populated forest of jack, white, and red pine, birch, and several types of shrubs. None are large because the site is harsh and the soil thin. As trees get taller, the wind eventually knocks them over, a fact to which the many downed trees here can attest.

When you emerge into the open, you'll be at the edge of a 60-foot drop into Lake Superior. The view is again wonderful. On a clear day you can see Wisconsin's Apostle Islands and the Bayfield Peninsula.

Make your way along the bare rock path to the last wooden platform and overlook. There is little vegetation here, as waves crash on these rocks and prevent much soil from sticking. Once you're on the wooden platform, let your eyes trace the 60- to 75-foot-high reddish cliffs that form the shoreline. They recede back into a cove before extending out to the northeast, where a series of similar shovel-like points juts out into the lake. At the cliff top, dark green conifers crowd the edge, with birch forming a soft white backdrop. At the cliff top, the eroded but still impressive contours of the Sawtooth Mountains backdrop the scene. In the water below, rainbow trout and some salmon ply

Legend

Parking	P
Trail	—
Intersecting Trail	
Park Office	
View	

the cold clearness, somehow managing to survive. Locals claim this is a good fishing spot.

When you've seen enough, hike back off the platform and stay right. A path winds along the cove edge for a few hundred feet and leads to a nature trail sign entitled "A Tiny Berry." It describes the lingonberry, a diminutive member of the blueberry family, that grows profusely around the sign and along the next 40 feet of trail. More common in arctic regions, the little berries from these plants are often called for in Norwegian recipes.

The rest of the hike is back along the trail you arrived here on. Retrace your steps to the wooden sign that directs you to either Shovel Point or to the beach. This time head toward the beach. There are a total of 94 steps plus some downhill pitches on the way there, so if you're tired you may want to reconsider. And don't expect a sandy beach reminiscent of a South Seas island, because you'll be disappointed.

What you'll find at the bottom of the last flight of 38 steps is a rocky cove about as big as a small house. The beach is covered with boulders, from beach ball to armchair size. Each is somehow different, not only in size but also in shape and color and, most strikingly, texture. Some are pitted, some fractured, some smooth as glass.

If you make a hard left at the base of the steps, you'll see another group of seven steps. Climb these and you'll reach a path that leads to another, bigger cove. At the point where you enter the cove, the beach is composed mostly of pebbles, pinhead to hardball sized, all mostly round, all in the eons-long process of being transformed into sand. They are loose and crunchy underfoot, louder and less responsive to moving feet than sand. Across the water, the opposite side of the cove is a sheer rock wall, 50-feet high, that tapers downhill, like a mini Shovel Point, to an end that juts out into Lake Superior. Unlike Shovel Point, this piece of rock ends in an arch, the one you saw earlier from the second overlook.

Walk across the beach toward the rock wall on the other side, and you'll notice that the pebbles have become softball- to bowling-ball-sized rocks. The wave action not only erodes these rocks into their round shapes but also efficiently sorts them by size into groups. Near the waterline, under the rocky cliff, sharper-edged hunks of rock, having fallen from the cliff side, await their turn to be rounded and sorted.

Finally, look for one of the massive logs that frequently wash up on the rocky beach. Debarked by constant pounding on the rocky shoreline, they lay tan and naked, with knobs where limbs had been. They are a wonderful spots for resting before heading up all those stairs and back to the parking lot.

Pothole Trail
Interstate State Park

Distance: Less than 1 mile

Time: 30 minutes, but it could be a lot longer if you become engrossed with the area's geologic curiosities.

Path: Mostly rocks and man-made wooden steps with some crushed rock in between. There are a lot of short climbs and descents.

Directions: The park entrance is directly across from the intersection of Highways 8 and 95 in Taylors Falls and just west of the Highway 8 bridge over the St. Croix River.

Contact: Interstate State Park, P.O. Box 254, Taylors Falls, MN 55084; (651)465-5711.

Highlights: Of all the geological wonders you'll encounter in Minnesota, the potholes you'll see at this park are perhaps the oddest and most awe inspiring.

Understanding the geologic history of the features that gave Pothole Trail its name and its fame is important if you are to truly appreciate them. A billion years ago (give or take a few million) major cracks developed in the earth's crust on a line from roughly Lake Superior's north shore down through Taylors Falls, the Twin Cities, and all the way to what is now Iowa. Lava spewed from these cracks, covering the land to a depth of a mile or more. Evidence of seven different lava flows can be found in the rock (basalt) near Taylors Falls.

The present-day Interstate State Park, both the river gorge and the potholes, was created near the end of the last glacial period, about 15,000 years ago. Back then, the entire St. Croix Basin in which the park is now situated was underwater, as massive amounts of ice in the north melted and glacial Lake Duluth began to overflow. The torrent carried more water than any modern-day river and was perhaps the largest river that ever flowed across the face of the earth.

All this water swirling southward carried boulders, sand, and gravel along with it. The sand and gravel got trapped in whirlpools and eddies, scoured the hard basalt rock, and formed bowl-like depressions. As the process continued, the bowls got deeper and the eddies got stronger. The water could then move even bigger rocks that fell into the current. These rocks, some bigger than bowling balls, ground away at the bottom of the bowls until either the river changed channel or its level dropped. What was left are the potholes that you'll see today.

Start your walk from the southeastern tip of the parking lot just past the visitor center. Take the trail that bears to the left. You'll first walk past several "baby potholes" that have been gouged into the hard bedrock. Continue out onto the bare rock ledges until you reach the first big pothole on your right. It's called Lilly Pond because it collects water and could grow lilies; usually it's filled with algae.

Continue southward toward the St. Croix River and you'll cross a fenced rock plateau that leads to a fenced walkway over an rock arch leading out to Angle Rock. If you're careful, you can climb up to the pinnacle of the rock and see upriver to the rapids just below the Highway 8 bridge. Note how the river makes an almost 90-degree right turn at Angle Rock. Like many other rivers in Minnesota, the St. Croix was a major conduit for logs back in the halcyon days of the

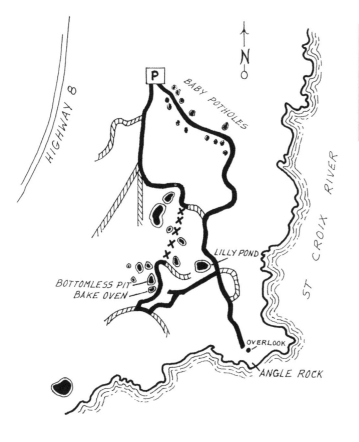

lumber industry. Sometimes the logs would get stuck in this bend. In June 1886, what may have been the world's largest logjam backed up an estimated 160 million board feet of logs 3 miles upstream. It took 200 men and uncounted sticks of dynamite six weeks to free the logs.

Head back to the potholes by retracing your steps over the arch. Near the end of the fenced area, bear left and walk under another stone arch, where you'll arrive at the Devil's Parlor. Notice the repeating concave nature of the high stone walls around you. This area was created when individual potholes merged.

Continue along the wooden steps and then the gray crushed-rock path through Devil's Parlor to the Bake Oven. There is a metal grate and stairway here that you can use to descend into a pothole. When you get to the bottom, make sure you touch the smooth rock side of the pothole and look up from the bottom to see the sky.

Once out of the pothole, climb the hand-hewn rock steps to the top of the pothole you were just inside. Walk around the iron fence and look at the adjacent pothole, which is named the Bottomless Pit, because during excavation diggers wondered if they would ever find a bottom. They did, 67.5 feet from the top. There are several unexcavated potholes in the park, and speculation has it that some of them may be even deeper.

Spend some time exploring the many side trails and unmarked potholes in this area of the park. When you're finished, head back north, away from Angle Rock and you'll reach a walkway that goes back to the parking area.

MORE GREAT TITLES FROM TRAILS BOOKS